Evangelistic Praying

Evangelistic Praying

Intercession for Laborers
and the Lost

Frank R. Shivers

LIGHTNING SOURCE
1246 Heil Quaker Blvd.
La Vergne, TN

Unless otherwise noted, Scripture quotations are from
The Holy Bible *King James Version*

Library of Congress Cataloging-in-Publication Data

Shivers, Frank R., 1949-
Evangelistic Praying / Frank Shivers
ISBN 978-1-878127-33-4

Library of Congress Control Number:
2017918798

Cover design by
Tim King of Click Graphics, Inc.

For Information:
Frank Shivers Evangelistic Association
P. O. Box 9991
Columbia, South Carolina 29290
www.frankshivers.com

Presented to

_____

By

_____

Date

_____

The real business of your life as a saved soul is intercessory prayer.[1]

~ Oswald Chambers

When we give in to laziness, moments of prayer that are missed can never be redeemed.[2]

~ Frederick W. Robertson

The powerful truth is, our prayers are being used to send laborers into the harvest.[3] ~ David Wilkerson

True prayer is neither a mere mental exercise nor a vocal performance. It is far deeper than that—it is spiritual transaction with the Creator of Heaven and Earth.[4] ~ C. H. Spurgeon

Now, if we—here in this so-called Christian country—really believed in prayer, i.e., in our Lord's own gracious promises, should we avoid prayer meetings? If we had any genuine concern for the lost condition of thousands in our own land and tens of thousands in heathen lands, should we withhold our prayers? Surely we do not think, or we should pray more. "Ask of me, I will give," says an almighty, all-loving God (Mark 6:23), and we scarcely heed His words![5] ~ Unknown

There is an Advocate and Intercessor always waiting to present the prayers of those who come to God through Him. That advocate is Jesus Christ. He mingles our prayers with the incense of His own almighty intercession. So mingled, they go up as a sweet savor before the throne of God. Poor as they are in themselves, they are mighty and powerful in the hand of our High Priest and Elder Brother. The banknote without a signature at the bottom is nothing but a worthless piece of paper. The stroke of a pen confers on it all its value. The prayer of a poor child of Adam is a feeble thing in itself, but once endorsed by the hand of the Lord Jesus it avails much.[6] ~ J. C. Ryle

To

Glen and Deborah Hughes

and Elizabeth Young

Helpers in the harvest

The Bible is indeed God's casebook, a record of His actions for the salvation of mankind. The stamp of the missionary purpose is on its every part.[7]

~William Carver

Contents

Preface

This little volume was birthed from study, prayer, research and much meditation for a sermon to be preached at an associational prayer event. Frankly those days forever changed the content, consistency and intensity of my praying. C. H. Spurgeon said that Matthew 9:38 weighed on his heart more than any other text in the Bible, that it haunted him perpetually.[8] The same now is true for me.

Evangelistic Praying by design is short and simple, in hope that it may be read and applied at one sitting and resorted to often. The time taken to soak in its contents will bring clarity and comprehension to the message, meaning and application of Jesus' words to believers in Matthew 9:38 when He states, "Pray ye therefore the Lord of the harvest, that he will send forth laborers into his harvest."

The fields are white unto harvest while the laborers are few in nearly every nook and cranny of the earth. The means in which laborers are supplied in these places is from Christians like yourself who pray them out of schools, colleges, churches, seminaries and secular work. It's not the praying that calls them; that's the Lord of the Harvest's task. However, it's the praying that moves God's hand to "send" them into His harvest.

Evangelistic praying works, for it is the divinely appointed and authorized means of Jesus for the placement of laborers according to their spiritual giftedness and skills wherein they are needed the most. In making evangelistic praying a priority, you will play a big part in the dispatching of laborers to various mission posts of the world and the conversion of the unsaved. Outside of soul winning, it may well be the greatest work the Christian will ever undertake.

– Chapter One –

Precept

Pray that the Master's Word will simply take off and race through the country to a groundswell of response, just as it did among you.
~ 2 Thessalonians 3:1 MSG

The Lord frequently taught His disciples that they must pray, and how, but seldom what to pray. But here (Matthew 9:38) we have one thing He expressly enjoins them to remember: in view of the plenteous harvest, and the need of reapers, they must cry to the Lord of the harvest to send forth laborers.[9] ~ Andrew Murray

Prayer is the gymnasium of the soul.[10] ~ Missionary Samuel Zwemer

So often we pray narrowly, attending only to our own needs. Instead, we should pray broadly for everyone. We should pray for the lost that they might be saved and for the saved that they might win the lost.[11] ~ D. James Kennedy

Do not we rest in our day too much on the arm of the flesh? Cannot the same wonders be done now as of old? Do not the eyes of the Lord run to and fro throughout the whole earth still to show Himself strong on behalf of those who put their trust in Him? Oh, that God would give me more practical faith in Him! Where is the Lord God of Elijah? He is waiting for Elijah to call on Him.[12] ~ James Gilmour

What is prayer? The prolific writer upon the subject of prayer, E. M. Bounds, said, "Prayer is the helpless and needy child crying to the compassion of the Father's heart and the bounty and power of a Father's hand."[13] John Stott said that "prayer is not a convenient device for imposing our will upon God or for bending His will to ours, but the prescribed way of subordinating our will to His. It is by prayer that we seek God's will, embrace it and align ourselves with it. Every true prayer is a variation on the theme, 'Your will be done.'"[14] A. T. Pierson said, "Prayer is the imparted power from God, and nothing else can take its place."[15]

In his sermon upon the text of Ezekiel 36:37, C. H. Spurgeon gave a definition and description of prayer: "Prayer, then, is an inquiry. No man

Evangelistic Praying

can pray aright, unless he views prayer in that light. First, I inquire what the promise is. I turn to my Bible, and I seek to find the promise whereby the thing which I desire to seek is certified to me as being a thing which God is willing to give. Having inquired so far as that, I take that promise, and on my bended knees I inquire of God whether He will fulfill His own promise. I take to Him His own word of covenant, and I say to Him, "O Lord, wilt Thou not fulfill it, and wilt Thou not fulfill it now?" So that there, again, prayer is inquiry. After prayer I look out for the answer. I expect to be heard, and if I am not answered I pray again, and my repeated prayers are but fresh inquiries. I expect the blessing to arrive."[16]

Chuck Swindoll said prayer "includes praise and thanksgiving, intercession and petition, meditation, and confession. In prayer, we focus fully on God, we capture renewed zeal to continue, we gain a wider view of life, and we obtain an increased determination to endure."[17]

Perhaps the simplest and most concise definition of prayer is stated by the theologian Matthew Henry: "The Bible is a letter God has sent to us; prayer is a letter we send to Him."[18]

One day the five-year-old son of the great evangelist D. L. Moody entered into his dad's study where he was busy writing and didn't want to be interrupted. The child simply stood beside him without making a sound. Finally, Moody gruffly said, "Well, what do you want?"

"Nothing, Daddy," said his son. "I just wanted to be where you are." The boy then sat on the floor quietly amusing himself. He only desired the companionship of his father.

G. Campbell Morgan, the gifted English minister, remarked that it was "this little incident, told by Mr. Moody, that helped me greatly understand the true meaning of prayer. To pray is to be where Jesus is. When we are in His presence, we need nothing more to pray prevailingly."[19]

The Private Prayer

To enter into one's closet and pray (Matthew 6:6) is to entertain the presence of Almighty God in secret. Words cannot capture the awesomeness of time spent alone in His presence. But perhaps Thomas Brooks, a nonconformist Puritan preacher, comes closest. He says, "A husband imparts his mind most freely and fully to his wife when she is alone; and so does Christ to the believing soul. Oh...the secret kisses, the secret embraces, the secret visits, the secret whispers, the secret cheerings, the

Precept

secret sealings, the secret discoveries which God gives to His people when in secret prayer."[20]

Shut in with God in the secret place,
There in the Spirit beholding His face,
Gaining new power to run in the race,
I love to be shut in with God.

Of all pleasant places on land or on sea,
There's no place on earth that is sweeter to me
Than to kneel at the feet of my Master and Lord,
For there I'll be shut in with God. ~ Unknown

Brooks further comments, "There is no service wherein Christians have such near and familiar intercourse with God as in this of private prayer. God crowns private prayer with a discovery of those blessed and weighty truths to His servants that are a sealed book to others."[21] This truth is borne out by Jesus following the discourse upon prayer (John 15:5). In John 15:15 He says, "Henceforth I call you not servants; for the servant knoweth not what his lord doeth: but I have called you friends; for all things that I have heard of my Father I have made known unto you." The psalmist said, "The secret of the LORD is with them that fear him" (Psalm 25:14).

The Public Prayer

Praying together as believers is biblical—Jesus (John 11:41–42), Solomon (1 Kings 8:22–23), Ezra (Ezra 10:1), Elijah (1 Kings 17:36–37), Paul (Acts 20:36), believers in the house of Mary (Acts 12:12). And there are various occasions for it—Sunday church prayer (invocation, offertory, pastoral, invitational); family prayer; Wednesday prayer meeting prayer; prayer band prayers (believers who pray together regularly); pastor- or layman-led prayer in the home; dedication prayer; prayer opening sessions of Congress or other governmental agencies.

In *Lectures to My Students,* C. H. Spurgeon speaks regarding the public prayer. He states, "Habitual communion with God must be maintained, or our public prayers will be vapid [i.e., flat or dull] or formal. If there be no melting of the glacier high up in the ravines of the mountain, there will be no descending rivulets to cheer the plain. Private prayer is the drill

Evangelistic Praying

ground for our more public exercises; neither can we long neglect it without being out of order when before the people."[22]

> Prayer is the highest and most blessed privilege afforded to the saint by God, but sadly the most neglected and abused.

Spurgeon then sternly cautions: "Beware of having an eye to the auditors; beware of becoming rhetorical to please the listeners. Prayer must not be transformed into an 'oblique sermon.' It is little short of blasphemy to make devotion an occasion for display....Remember the people in your prayers, but do not mold your supplications to win their esteem."[23] He then advised ministers "to preach in the sermon and pray in the prayer."[24]

Don't shortchange public prayer, but at the same time don't injure it by praying too long. "He prayed me into a good frame of mind," George Whitefield once said of a certain preacher, "and if he had stopped there, it would have been very well; but he prayed me out of it again by keeping on."[25]

Thus in a nutshell, prayer (private and public) is simply approaching God with a clean and submissive heart for the purpose of conversing with Him (praise, adoration, worship, thanksgiving); requesting of Him (based upon His promises and in accordance with His will) and receiving from Him (spiritually, physically and materialistically). Prayer is the highest and most blessed privilege afforded to the saint by God, but sadly the most neglected and abused.

A Christian died and went to Heaven. In his tour of the Celestial City he saw a huge warehouse stuffed with boxes and packages of various shapes and sizes that stretched for miles. He learned that in the boxes and packages were unrequested prayers, answers to prayers God was ready to send but which were not requested. This fictitious story illustrates James' words, "Ye have not, because ye ask not" (4:2). The main culprit behind unanswered prayers is unoffered prayers.

Evangelistic Praying

Among the things which the believer is to request in prayer, Jesus exhorts him to pray specifically for laborers for the harvest and the unsaved. He said, "The harvest truly is plenteous, but the laborers are few; Pray ye therefore the Lord of the harvest, that he will send forth laborers

Precept

into his harvest" (Matthew 9:37–38).

John Gill comments, "This is the petition the disciples of Christ were put upon making to the Lord of the harvest, on consideration of the present condition multitudes of souls were in. They could not make, qualify and send out ministers themselves; this is not man's work, but God's. He only is able to furnish with ministerial gifts, to work upon and powerfully incline the hearts of men to this service, to call and send them forth into it, and to assist and succeed them in it. The…place they are desired to be sent into is 'into the harvest,' into the field of the world…and there labor in preaching the Gospel, hoping…for the conversion of sinners and edification of saints."[26]

A farmer's fine crop of grain was destroyed by a turbulent storm. Crops on neighboring farms had been harvested into the barn prior to the storm and were spared. The farmer of the field sadly stood in silence observing the ruined harvest. A passerby walked up to the farmer and said, "It is a sad sight, isn't it?"

The farmer replied, "You would really think it was a sad sight if it were your field. I could not get anyone to help me harvest the crops."

That sounds a whole lot like what Jesus said in Matthew 9:38. A *great storm* is approaching (the condemnation of God upon sin and the sinner), and the ready harvest must be gathered into the barn lest it be lost. The Lord of the harvest, seeing the shortage of workers in the field, has sent out a plea for more help. Will believers respond to the cry, or will He say at the judgment, "I could not get anyone to help Me harvest the field, therefore many were lost"?

> The bottom line is that fervent evangelistic praying for laborers is crucial because it is God's ordained method for their recruitment within and outside the church and assures Holy Spirit appointees in contrast to man's.

"Ask" (Matthew 7:7) is the believer's instruction to cause God's desired purpose for laborers among the lost in every tribe and nation to be fulfilled and to bring about their conversion. The bottom line is that fervent evangelistic praying for laborers is crucial because it is God's ordained method for their recruitment within and outside the church and assures Holy Spirit appointees in contrast to man's.

Evangelistic Praying

It is said of John Hyde (Praying Hyde), missionary to India, that "he prayed as if God was at his elbow, standing ready to answer. He had faith." Pray specifically (identify places, people, positions by name as much as possible) and believingly for laborers to be sent forth into the harvest and for the lost to be saved.

Chapter Two

Purpose

The wheels of all machinery for extending the Gospel are moved by prayer.[27] ~ J. C. Ryle

It must be our prayer that the Lord would fill all His people with the spirit of devotion, so that no one may be found standing idle in the vineyard. Wherever there is a complaint about the lack of fit helpers for God's work, prayer has the promise of a supply. God is always ready and able to provide. It may take time and importunity, but Christ's command to ask the Lord of the harvest is the pledge that the prayer will be heard. "I say unto you...he will rise and give him as many as he needeth" (Luke 11:8).[28] ~ Andrew Murray

God does nothing except in response to believing prayer.[29] ~ John Wesley

Did Jesus ever tell His disciples to pray that the unsaved would begin following Him? Of course not. He did say, however, "Pray ye therefore the Lord of the harvest, that he will send forth laborers into his harvest" (Matthew 9:38). Prayer then is to be used to get the saved awakened to the lostness of the lost.[30] ~ Bailey Smith

If you are a Christian, then you are God's watchman unto the world. "Son of man, I have made thee a watchman unto the house of Israel: therefore hear the word at my mouth, and give them warning from me. When I say unto the wicked, Thou shalt surely die; and thou givest him not warning, nor speakest to warn the wicked from his wicked way, to save his life; the same wicked man shall die in his iniquity; but his blood will I require at thine hand" (Ezekiel 3:17–18).

Watchmen were stationed in tall towers along the fences of cities in Old Testament times to watch for and give warning of approaching enemies. If the watchman failed in his duty and citizens died as a result, then he would be held accountable (their blood would be on his hands). God used this symbolism to declare to us, "Son of man, I have appointed you a watchman" (Ezekiel 3:17 Darby).

Evangelistic Praying

Similarly, in Hebrews God's ministers are described as those who "watch for your souls" (Hebrews 13:17). What is it to watch for souls? It is to warn of the consequences of sin and point out the only escape from it. It is to be vigilant in prayer vigils, interceding for the lost and for ministry laborers to populate the land. It is to be indefatigable and persistent in going to the lost with the Good News. It is to safeguard the believer, lest he stumble spiritually. "Laziness and frivolity," says J. C. Ryle, "are bad enough in any profession but worst of all in that of a watchman for souls."[31]

Penetrating the lostness in North America and throughout the world which tops four billion people will require multiple thousands of watchmen [church planters, evangelists, pastors, missionaries and soul winners]. Whence will these come to work in the harvest? Jesus states they will *come* from evangelistic praying. Believers are to pray them out into the field.

Evangelistic Praying Includes Laborers

Christianity has labor trouble. Jesus said "The harvest truly is plenteous, but the laborers are few." The labor shortage says Jesus is to be remedied through praying "the Lord of the harvest." Oswald J. Smith remarked, "The problem is still one of laborers. If we had a sufficient number of laborers, the job could be done, but we have always been short-handed. We must get more laborers."[32]

E. M. Bounds states, "Missionaries, like ministers, are born of praying people. A praying church begets laborers in the harvest field of the world. The scarcity of missionaries argues a non-praying church."[33] Pray for pastors, associate ministers, musicians and singers, evangelists, Bible translators, church planters and missionaries to be raised up and utilized in fulfilling the Great Commission. Likewise pray for layman to be raised up to teach, testify, train and preach at home and abroad. Pray more of them into volunteer missions and the work of soul winning. Pray for the persecuted church and its need for laborers in places like North Korea which has been ranked the most oppressive place in the world for Christians for 16 years.

Pray for native laborers to be raised up and sent out into their own land. A missionary magazine addressed the need for multitudes of native workers in the unreached territories of the world. Upon reading the article, one would think it was written yesterday, when in fact it was published in

Purpose

1847. Sadly, the need for native ministers and missionaries is greater today than it was then. In part the article states:

"Is it said that native laborers must be employed? But where are the native laborers? Not every native convert is fitted, or can be fitted, to this work. And of those whom the Spirit may call to the ministry, what training of mind and heart and life is prerequired. There must be native laborers, but they must be called and sanctified; they must be made intelligent and wise; they must not be novices, but well-instructed, 'faithful men, who shall be able to teach others also' (2 Tim. 2:2). These native laborers cannot be adequately trained, and in sufficient number, independently of the general culture of the community around them. The whole native mass of ignorance and corruption, in some degree at least, must needs be enlightened and purified. New thoughts, new motives, new pursuits, new habits and customs, a higher order of being and acting, must be given to the general mind; and from this higher level of the national mind must be reared, as in Christian lands, a native ministry. Who shall perform this stupendous labor? Who will educate the people?"[34]

The church must pray specifically both for additional native laborers (conversion and calling out) and missionaries (to train, instruct them as to how to be a harvester of souls).

Your church (and the entire harvest field) will have more laborers if you intentionally pray for them. The shortage of laborers is directly linked to the shortage of prayers for them.

> Your church (and the entire harvest field) will have more laborers if you intentionally pray for them.

Dr. John R. Rice stated, "The Lord Jesus said distinctly in Matthew 9:35–38, and again in Luke 10:2, that 'the harvest truly is plenteous [or great], but the laborers are few'; and He said that we should 'pray...therefore the Lord of the harvest, that he would send forth laborers into his harvest.' Then surely fathers and mothers should pray that God will call their sons to be great soul winners. Would it not be proper for them to pray that God would raise them up as mighty, Spirit-filled evangelists? And would it not be proper for young men to pray that God would send them into the harvest as evangelists? I think so."[35] But with that said, Matthew Poole offers a word of caution: "None ought to thrust themselves into the work of the ministry till God thrust them out, Hebrews 5:4."[36]

Evangelistic Praying

"The real need," says Dr. Bailey Smith," is not to pray for souls but soul winners."[37] He explains, "The most effective praying is not for the lost world but rather for the saved to have a concern for the world that's lost. Prayer then is to be used to get the saved awakened to the lostness of the lost."[38]

Robert Coleman in *The Master Plan for Evangelism* said, "There is no use to pray for the world. What good would it do? God already loves them and has given His Son to save them. No, there is no use to pray vaguely for the world. The world is lost and blind in sin. The only hope for the world is for laborers to go to them with the Gospel of salvation, and having won them to the Savior, not to leave them but to work with them faithfully, patiently, painstakingly until they become fruitful Christians savoring the world about them with the Redeemer's love."[39]

C. H. Spurgeon elucidates: "The Gospel will not be revealed to men by any supernatural agency; we must go with it. They cannot learn it without being taught it. No man will know the Gospel unless somebody shall tell it to him by word of mouth or by the gift of a book or a tract or by a letter or by the open preaching of the Word."[40]

Evangelistic praying for the lost certainly has great value (Smith, Coleman and Spurgeon agree) but in and of itself cannot be the means of salvation for any soul who has never been presented the Gospel. It can open blind eyes and deaf ears and destroy barriers in man's pathway to salvation, but ultimately a witness (laborer) must declare unto them the death, burial and resurrection of Jesus if they are to be saved. Paul said, "How can they believe in the one of whom they have not heard? And how can they hear without someone preaching to them?" (Romans 10:14 NIV). And it is for these workers to be raised up and sent out that believers must pray.

Why the Lack of Laborers?

Jack Hyles well said, "An army officer may need reinforcing troops. He calls headquarters and requisitions more men, and the reinforcements are sent. The troops are there waiting to be sent. Headquarters is waiting for the requisition. Pastors all across America and around the world lament the fact that they have so few workers, and yet they never make requisition. They never call headquarters and ask for workers! How sad, how sad, how sad it is that we go without laborers when the Lord of the harvest has them available and waiting for us, but we do not ask for them! The difference

Purpose

between the church that has soul winners and the church that doesn't have soul winners is prayer. The difference between the church that [has sufficient Sunday school teachers and the church that] has a scarcity of Sunday school teachers is prayer. God has the laborers. He wants us to have them. He wants to send them, but somehow Christian leaders have a trace of atheism in them. We somehow do not believe that God will supply our needs in answer to our requests, so we set out to connive and plan with our human reasoning to get workers 'by hook or by crook.'"[41]

A Prayer for Laborers

Lord of the harvest, hear
Thy needy servants cry;
Answer our faith's effectual prayer
And all our wants supply.

On Thee we humbly wait;
Our wants are in Thy view:
The harvest truly, Lord, is great;
The laborers are few.

Convert and send forth more
Into Thy church abroad,
And let them speak Thy word of power
As workers with their God.

Give the pure Gospel Word,
The word of glorious grace;
Thee let them preach, the only Lord
And Savior of our race.

Oh, let them spread Thy name,
Their mission fully prove,
Thy condescending grace proclaim,
Thine all-redeeming love! ~ Charles Wesley

Some may say that Jesus' words are not applicable to our day. After all, there appear to be far more laborers than what is needed. However, prior to contradicting Jesus, they had better realize that He knows more than they know and that's why He said what He did. Here's the point I believe Jesus is making. We have many laborers but few sanctified and

Evangelistic Praying

otherwise qualified laborers. Many laborers in the church or mission field peddle that which is scriptural perversion, or they are just plain lackadaisical with regard to their work in the harvest field. The nation of Israel had her share of spiritually destitute shepherds or laborers. Jeremiah, among other prophets, denounced them, saying, "Woe to the shepherds who destroy and scatter the sheep of My pasture" (Jeremiah 23:1 HCSB)! That denouncement still stands.

So it's not just any sort of *laborers* that are needed in the field. What kind of laborers are we to pray will be supplied? C. H. Spurgeon gives answer: "We need laborers, not loiterers. We need men on fire, and I beseech you, pray to God to send them. The harvest can never be reaped by men who will not labor. They must be off with their coats and go at it in their shirtsleeves—I mean they must doff their dignities and get to Christ's work as if they meant it, like real harvest men. They must sweat at their work, for nothing in the harvest field can be done without the sweat of the face, or in the pulpit without the sweat of the soul."[42]

John Gill, in his commentary upon Matthew 9:38, underscores Spurgeon's description of the laborers for which we are to pray: "The persons desired to be sent are 'laborers'; faithful, diligent, and industrious preachers [laymen and vocational ministers] of the Gospel; such as lay out themselves, their time, talents and strength in their master's service and do not indulge themselves in sloth and idleness."[43]

The church and mission field have many workers of the ordinary brand who profit the kingdom extremely little. Pray for the extraordinary brand, laborers who are Spirit-filled, sold-out, zealous, doctrinally sound and evangelistic minded to be raised up in great numbers.

Talk to Students about Christian Service

All that has been stated does not relieve ministers, parents and teachers of the responsibility of *talking* to students about the possibility of Christian service. In fact, this ought to be done. Old-timers recall that years ago when placing long distance phone calls by landline, they could be made person-to-person or station-to-station. Primarily God extends a call to vocational Christian service Person-to-person, directly to the person. However, sometimes it is extended station-to-station, through another person. It was my mother who spoke to me about the possibility of vocational Christian service while I was a junior in high school.

Purpose

Dr. G. Allen Fleece commented, "Unless God has made it perfectly clear in some way that He does not want you on the mission field, every young Christian should face in that direction and hold the matter before God until He either leads out to the field or closes the door by a call to other service."[44]

Evangelistic Praying Includes the Unsaved

The context of Jesus' words regarding Matthew 9:38 underscores the need for believers to pray for the unsaved. John MacArthur says, "Whether friend or foe, whether moral or immoral, whether you know them or not—pray for the lost."[45] Courtland Myers states, "Jesus' greatest agency in winning men back to Himself is the prayer of other men."[46] Praying for the lost to be gloriously saved is biblical.

Moses prayed for the lost. "Pardon, I beseech thee, the iniquity of this people according unto the greatness of thy mercy, and as thou hast forgiven this people, from Egypt even until now" (Numbers 14:19).

Jeremiah prayed for the lost. How do we know? On one occasion following a great sin committed by the people, God said to him, "Therefore pray not thou for this people, neither lift up cry nor prayer for them, neither make intercession to me: for I will not hear thee" (Jeremiah 7:16). Obviously it had been Jeremiah's habit to cry out in behalf of the lost, for in this incident he is told not to do so.

Jesus prayed for the lost. "Father, forgive them; for they do not know what they are doing" (Luke 23:34 NASB).

Paul prayed for the lost. He said, "Brethren, my heart's desire and prayer to God for Israel is, that they might be saved" (Romans 10:1).

> God forbid that I should sin against the LORD in ceasing to pray for you.
> 1 Samuel 12:23

Stephen prayed for the lost. As he was being stoned, "He fell to his knees, shouting, "Lord, don't charge them with this sin!" And with that, he died" (Acts 7:60 NLT). If ever a man died in a "hurry," it was Stephen, and yet he made time to pray for the lost. The believer ought to earnestly say unto the lost, "God forbid that I should sin against the LORD in ceasing to pray for you" (1 Samuel 12:23).

Evangelistic Praying

They're passing, passing fast away,
A hundred thousand souls a day
    In Christless guilt and gloom.
O Church of Christ, what wilt thou say
When in the awful judgment day,
    They charge thee with their doom. ~ A. B. Simpson

How to Pray for the Lost

In Peter Lord's *29:59 Prayer Plan,* an unnamed writer summarizes how believers are to pray for the lost. She writes, "We should claim the tearing down of all the works of Satan, such as false doctrine, unbelief, atheistic teaching, and hatred which the Enemy may have built up in their thinking. We must pray that their very thoughts will be brought into captivity to the obedience of Christ. We should pray also that their conscience may be convicted, that God may bring them to the point of repentance, and that they may listen and believe as they hear or read the Word of God"[47] (2 Corinthians 10:4–5).

"Praying for the lost," states John MacArthur "should never be cold, detached or impersonal, like a public defender assigned to represent a defendant. Understanding the depths of their misery and pain, and their coming doom, we must cry to God for the salvation of sinners."[48]

The famous Baptist minister Dr. George Truett issues a solemn appeal to engage in intercessory prayer for the unsaved. He states, "We talk a great deal about our 'unanswered prayers.' Let us then rather think about our unoffered prayers. Your boy might have been saved if you had prayed as you ought. I declare it upon the authority of God's Book. Your husband might have been saved if you had prayed as you ought and lived rightly along with the praying. I declare it upon the authority of the same Book. Some man for whose soul you yearn might long ago have stood up in the presence of the people of God, saying, 'Your God is mine; your hope mine,' if you and I and all of us had prayed for that man as we ought. One of the deepest regrets of my life, I confess it to you today, is that I have prayed so little for lost sinners compared with what I ought to have prayed. O my people, our children, our loved ones, to an awful degree are dependent upon our prayers. And there are lost men…all about us; God forbid that we should so sin against the Lord as to cease praying for them."[49]

Purpose

Prayer and Man's Free Will

S. D. Gordon states, "Man is a free agent, to use the old phrase, so far as God is concerned—utterly, wholly free. *And* he is the most enslaved agent on earth, so far as sin and selfishness and prejudice are concerned. The purpose of our praying is not to force or coerce his will—never that. It is to *free* his will of the warping influences that now twist it awry. It is to get the dust out of his eyes so his sight shall be clear. And once he is free, able to see aright, to balance things without prejudice, the whole probability is in favor of his using his will to choose the only right."[50]

Obviously prayer cannot save a person, but it certainly can put the wheels in motion for his salvation. Joe Henry Hankins agrees, saying, "Praying can bring the power of God to convict a soul, can bring the Holy Spirit upon a lost soul, can move the feet of a lost man toward the house of God and work wonders in his salvation."[51]

> Prayer cannot save a person, but it certainly can put the wheels in motion for his salvation.

David Wilkerson wrestled with what *appeared* to be a conflict between prayer for the lost and man's free will. He said, "As a younger Christian, I was often confused by some teaching and preaching that said, in essence, 'God's Word cannot lie. If we ask *anything* in His name, He will do it. God is bound to His Word. He will answer us.' I believed this. However, when it came to praying for unsaved loved ones, I wondered about it in light of the teaching regarding the free will of man. I thought, *If my prayers can cause a person to turn to Christ, doesn't this trespass man's free will?* I have learned to accept both truths as being possible yet not contradictory. Through prayer, we can move men toward God. Through prayer, we can see our loved ones come to Christ. I also believe the unsaved have a free will of their own, and they may resist the conviction of the Holy Spirit which comes as a result of our prayers....We are to pray 'without ceasing' and leave the ultimate outcome in the hands of God and within the decision-making prerogative of the unsaved."[52]

Fish and Conant in *Every Member Evangelism for Today* state, "We advance in our evangelistic work in direct proportion to the time we spend on our knees. Prayer produces the atmosphere through which unbelievers can understand the Word, and unless they hear the Word, the Holy Spirit

Evangelistic Praying

is unable to illumine their blinded minds and convince their hearts that their need is Christ alone. Witnessing apart from prayer, no matter how convincing to the reason, or even how convicting to the conscience, may prove to be a 'savor of death unto death.' Prayer opens and prayerlessness closes the channel between some lost soul and God."[53]

Evangelistic Praying Includes Open Doors

The *doors* of some nations for missionaries to enter with the Gospel are closed, and others are closing (there is a *tightening* of things with regard to the Christian witness). Christians must pray for the *doors* that are shut to open and those that are open to remain so that the harvest may be gathered into the "barn." It is biblical to do so. Regardless of how closed a door may appear, God is more than able to thrust it open. If God can tear down the Iron Curtain in Europe and the Bamboo Curtain in Asia, nothing can prevent His opening of other "difficult" doors.[54]

Biblical Examples of Open Doors

The Apostle Paul urged the Colossian Christians, "And pray at the same time for us also, that God may open for us a door for preaching, for us to tell the truth concerning Christ for the sake of which I am even a prisoner" (Colossians 4:3 WNT). They did and doors to preach the Gospel were opened even while he was incarcerated. While a prisoner, boldly and without hindrance he preached the kingdom of God and taught about the Lord Jesus Christ (Acts 28:30–31).

The Apostle Peter was imprisoned. "But while Peter was in prison, the church prayed very earnestly for him" (Acts 12:5 NLT). The Greek word for "earnestly" means "they pleaded with all their heart; they stretched themselves out in prayer." God is pleased and honored with that kind of praying! In response to their praying, God opened the prison door, setting Peter free (Acts 12:6–10).

> Doors that are closed yet may open upon the hinges of prayer.

In the same miraculous way that God opened the door for the Iron Curtain in Europe, the Bamboo Curtain in Asia, and for Paul and Peter in response to prayer, He stands ready to open a closed door to the Gospel whether it be a person's heart or a nation's border in response to our prayers. Doors that are closed yet may open upon the hinges of prayer.

Chapter Three

Preparation

The conditions of prayer are well ordered and clear—abiding in Christ, in His name.[55] ~ E. M. Bounds

It is not enough to say a prayer, but we must *pray* in prayer. Our thoughts must be fixed, our desires firm and ardent, and our graces in exercise; and, when we thus pray in prayer, we shall speed in prayer.[56] ~ Matthew Henry

We're living in an unprecedented day when evil is no longer evil. We've changed the terminology—iniquity is now infirmity; wickedness is now weakness; devilry is now deficiency....We need a mighty avalanche of conviction of sin....Nobody else can give you a clean heart but God.[57] ~ Leonard Ravenhill

Words said without heart are as utterly useless to our souls as the drum beating of savages before their idols. Where there is no heart, there may be lip-work and tongue-work, but there is no prayer.[58] ~ J. C. Ryle

Jesus declared the heart condition for effective praying in John 15:7: "If ye abide in me, and my words abide in you, ye shall ask what ye will, and it shall be done unto you." Forthrightly He states that failure to walk in fellowship with Him hinders prayer. Therefore, preparation for evangelistic praying begins long before going to your knees. It entails continual heart devotion, discipline and duty for Jesus.

> We live in Him, by Him, for Him,
> to Him, when we abide in Him.
> C. H. Spurgeon

C. H. Spurgeon explains what it is to abide in Jesus. "We live in Him, by Him, for Him, to Him, when we abide in Him. We feel that all our separate life has gone, 'for ye are dead, and your life is hid with Christ' (Colossians 3:3). We are nothing if we get away from Jesus; we would then be branches withered and fit only to be cast into the fire. We have no reason for existence except that which we find in Christ."[59]

Evangelistic Praying

James McConkey expands Spurgeon's thought: "God's wonderful fact [is] that for the man or the woman who is abiding in Him, He stands ready to do their will, through prayer. Why should it not be so? When we ask God to do anything according to His will, why should He not do it? God is just as pleased to do that part of His will for which you ask as any part of His will in the universe. It is for the honor and glory and interest of God to do your will when you are asking according to His will. Out there on those great wheat farms in the western prairies, is not the owner ready to do the superintendent's will as well as the superintendent to do the owner's will? If the harvesting machine gets out of order and the superintendent asks for its repair, it is to the interest of the owner to repair it. If the grain is mildewed and spoiling and the superintendent asks for hands to harvest it, it is to the interest of the owner to answer his request."[60]

McConkey continues, "So when we live in His will and are striving to do His will, it is to the interest of God's own kingdom that that will be done, and it pleases God to do it. God is just waiting for us to choose His will. And when we choose to do His will and ask for anything according to it, He will do it. I tell you, the greatest thought about prayer is not that we are praying to God to do something for us, but that we are praying to God to carry out His will in this world of His. And when we pray that, God stands ready to carry it out."[61] It is such abiding that our Savior said was essential if our prayers were to be successful.

> If I regard iniquity in my heart, the
> Lord will not hear me.
> Psalm 66:18

Sins that hinder prayer must be removed out of the way through the blood of Christ (1 John 1:7). David said, "If I regard iniquity in my heart, the Lord will not hear me" (Psalm 66:18).

Sins that hinder prayer from being effective include disobedience (Micah 3:4; Deuteronomy 1:43–45; Jeremiah 11:10–11); arrogance (James 4:6–10; Job 35:12–13); hypocrisy (Mark 12:38–40; Matthew 15:1–9); refusal to help the poor (Proverbs 21:13); unconfessed sin (John 9:31; Isaiah 59:1–2; Psalm 66:18); unforgiving spirit (Mark 11:25); indifference toward the Word of God (Proverbs 28:9); and a wrong relationship with your spouse (1 Peter 3:7).

Preparation

W. A. Criswell stated that "disunity, disassociation, disagreement tear up our ableness to reach God in Heaven."[62] George Sweeting declared, "Sin in the believer's life makes prayer worthless."[63]

An employee who worked for a city located in a valley was fired. In anger the man plugged the primary pipe that supplied water to the city from the reservoir in the mountain. People fully expecting water to flow upon turning the nozzle or knob were sorely disappointed when nothing happened. Efforts to ascertain the cause were unsuccessful.

In time the distraught employee confessed to the act, indicating the place the channel or pipe was plugged. Upon removal of the plug, the water flowed freely again.

We wonder why we pray and little or nothing happens. It is because the channel or pipe between God and us has been clogged with some form of sin. The sin must be acknowledged and removed for the power of God to flow freely into us and for our prayers to have effect.

James says, "The effectual fervent prayer of a righteous man availeth much" (James 5:16). That is, pray from a righteous heart for your prayers to be extremely effective. How? By praying at the first: "Lord Jesus, I desire to recall, confess and forsake every sin that injures not only my prayer life but my fellowship with You. I wait upon you, dear Lord, for revelation of every sin, that I might be forgiven of them through Thy precious blood upon my confession and repentance" (see 1 John 1:9–10).

Holy Spirit, breathe on me
    Until my heart is clean;
Let sunshine fill its inmost part,
    With not a cloud between.

Breathe on me; breathe on me;
    Holy Spirit, breathe on me.
Take Thou my heart; cleanse every part.
    Holy Spirit, breathe on me. ~ B. B. McKinney

Though spoken over a century ago, the advice given by Bishop Hall regarding prayer is extremely timely. He stated, "Remember, the Lord will not hear you because of the arithmetic of your prayers, counting their

Evangelistic Praying

numbers. He will not hear you because of the rhetoric of your prayers, caring for the eloquent language in which they are conveyed. He will not listen because of the geometry of your prayers, computing them by their length or breadth. He will not regard you because of the music of your prayers, caring for sweet voices or for harmony. Neither will He look at you because of the logic of your prayers, because they are well arranged and excellently divided. But He will hear you, and He will measure the amount of blessings He will give you, according to the divinity of your prayers. If you can plead the person of Christ, and if the Holy Ghost inspires you with zeal and earnestness, the blessings that you shall ask shall surely come to you."[64]

"Each time before you intercede," states Andrew Murray, "be quiet first, and worship God in His glory. Think of what He can do and how He delights to hear the prayers of His redeemed people. Think of your place and privilege in Christ, and expect great things!"[65]

Chapter Four

Priority

Let the people praise thee, O God; let all the people praise thee. ~ Psalm 67:3

God's greatest agency in winning men back to himself is the prayer of other men. How few enter into the positive, practical power of prayer.[66] ~ Courtland Meyers

Prayer is not logical; it is a mysterious moral working of the Holy Spirit.[67] ~ Oswald Chambers

Man is at his greatest and highest when upon his knees he comes face to face with God.[68] ~ G. Campbell Morgan

How little Christians really feel and mourn the need of laborers in the fields of the world so white to the harvest. And how little they believe that our labor supply depends on prayer, that prayer will really provide 'as many as he needeth.'[69] ~ Andrew Murray

They love me best who love me in their prayers.[70] ~ J. C. Ryle

J esus said there is a crisis (emergency) in the harvest field. The fields are ripe for harvesting, but there is a shortage of laborers. Therefore, prayer for laborers must be at the top of our prayer lists. *Yet seldom, if ever, does it even make it to the prayer lists of most believers.*

Untold millions yet are untold. The IMB (International Mission Board of the Southern Baptist Convention) estimates that there are 11,741 people groups in the world. *People Group* is defined as "an ethnolinguistic group with a common self-identity that is shared by the various members."[71] Of these, 7,027 are *Unreached People Groups* (UPG— groups that are less than two percent evangelical Christian, that do not have indigenous believers who can carry the Gospel to the rest of their group). UPG's total 4.3 billion people, or 58.1 percent of the world's population. *Unengaged Unreached People Groups* (UUPG) number 3,179. These are those which have no access to the Gospel or church planting strategy. The population of the UUPG's are 220 million people.[72]

Evangelistic Praying

Engaged People Groups are those which have an outside Christian effort "actively pursuing a church planting strategy among them."[73] However, these groups are still considered "unreached groups" until they are able to facilitate church planting without outside help.[74]

Research reveals there is a difference of opinion on exactly how many UPG's exist, but all agree the number is excessively high. The need of more than four billion to hear the gospel message, some for the very first time, is paramount and urgent.

Largest Unreached People Groups in the World

1. Shaikh in Bangladesh	132,950,000
2. Japanese in Japan	121,950,000
3. Shaikh in India	73,079,000
4. Brahman in India	54,955,000
5. Yadava in India	54,272,000
6. Turk in Turkey	52,739,000
7. Chamar in India	48,011,000
8. Rajput in India	39,839,000
9. Han Chinese, Xiang in China	36,033,000
10. Sunda in Indonesia	35,105,000[75]

The 10/40 Window

The majority of unreached people groups live in places stretching across the map from West Africa to East Asia. This rectangular area or band was named "The 10/40 Window" (often called "The Resistant Belt") by mission strategist Luis Bush because it lies across Africa and Asia from 10 degrees latitude north to 40 degrees latitude north of the equator. Among the world's 50 least evangelized countries, 37 lie within this window. These countries comprise 97 percent of the total population of the 50.[76]

Nations in the 10/40 Window for which to pray for laborers.

Afghanistan	Algeria	Bahrain	Bangladesh
Benin	Bhutan	Burkina Faso	Cambodia
Chad	China	Cyprus	Djibouti
Egypt	Eritrea	Ethiopia	Gambia
Gibraltar	Greece	Guinea	Guinea-Bissau
India	Iran	Iraq	Israel
Japan	Jordan	Korea, North	Korea, South
Kuwait	Laos	Lebanon	Libya

Priority

Macau	Mali	Malta	Mauritania
Morocco	Myanmar (Burma)	Nepal	Niger
Oman	Pakistan	Philippines	Portugal
Qatar	Saudi Arabia	Senegal	Sudan

In excess of one thousand unreached people groups (eighty million people) are *not* in the 10/40 Window.[77]

The Bibleless People Groups of the World

Fifty-seven percent of the world's languages need Bible translations. The Barna Research State of the Bible Survey (2015) revealed that seventy-two percent of Christians believe the Gospel is available in all the world's languages. However, this is not the case, for 1,860 language groups do not even have Scripture portions, much less the entire Bible, available in their primary language. Four thousand five hundred language groups comprising a billion people do not have a full Bible.[78] Though progress is being made—the entire Bible is now available in 636 different languages to more than 5.135 billion people[79]—much remains to be done by presently so few translators.

People Dying Without Jesus Christ

The estimated number of people that perish without the Gospel in America and around the world: 1.68 per second, 101 per minute, 6,048 per hour, and 145,000 per day.

Understanding the times and the urgency for the harvest, I paraphrase David's words to Ahimelech in 1 Samuel 21:8: 'The King's business requireth haste.' Let us redeem the time by praying strenuously and laboriously for workers to be thrust into the fields in the regions beyond and next door. Especially pray for laborers to be summoned by the Lord to enter places and preach Christ where the light of the Gospel has never shone.

Oswald J. Smith said, "We talk of the Second Coming; half the world has never heard of the first. No one has the right to hear the Gospel twice while there remains someone who has not heard it once."[80]

John Calvin, in his commentary on Matthew 9:38, writes: "There never was greater necessity for offering this prayer than during the fearful desolation of the church which we now see everywhere around us."[81] If "fearful desolation of the church" existed in Calvin's day, how much more does it exist in ours, prompting urgency in praying for laborers.

Evangelistic Praying

Rev. Motte Martin of Africa tells of one who sought a missionary for his distant village. He was thrice refused, being told, "You must wait. There is no one to send."

Brokenhearted, he cried out, "How long must we wait? Oh, Teacher, ask the white man in your land how long we must wait." The story led to the writing of the hymn "How Long Must We Wait?" Envision natives in third-world countries voicing the plea it cites.

Long have we sought eternal life;
Years have we waited in sin and strife,
In darkness groped, sad misery's mate.
How long? how long must we wait?

How long? how long must we wait?
How long? how long must we wait?
The lab'rers still are few;
Our Lord has need of you.
How long? how long must we wait?

We must pray laborers into such places in our world. Of the 4.19 million full-time Christian workers, ninety-five percent are working within the Christian world.[82] There is most assuredly a crisis for laborers in the non-Christian world, but their need in North America also is escalating.

The nations call! From sea to sea
    Extends the thrilling cry,
"Come over, Christians, if there be,
    And help us, ere we die."

Our hearts, O Lord, the summons feel;
    Let hand and heart combine
And answer to the world's appeal
    By giving "that is thine."[83] ~ Ann Taylor

Chapter Five

Power

This power has been given to us in prayer to provide in the need of the world, to secure the servants for God's work. The Lord of the harvest will hear. Christ, who called us so specially to pray thus, will support our prayers offered in His name and interest.[84] ~ Andrew Murray

When we pray with confidence and commitment, we can expect God to bring the glorious consequences of His Spirit being received, unity being achieved, and the Gospel being believed.[85] ~ Adrian Rogers

Take Christ's Word (His promise) and Christ's sacrifice (His blood) with you to the throne of grace through prayer, and not one of Heaven's blessings can be denied you.[86] ~ Adam Clarke

There is power in evangelistic praying, for Jesus authorized it, commanded it, and promised to answer it. Our prayers move the Holy Spirit into action, resulting in laborers being sent out and souls being saved.

God's mightiest saints attest to the power of evangelistic praying. *Andrew Murray* says, "The number of missionaries on the field is entirely dependent on someone praying out laborers." Again, he states, "So wonderful is the surrender of His work into the hands of His church, so dependent has the Lord made Himself on them as His body, through whom alone His work can be done, so real is the power which the Lord gives His people to exercise in Heaven and earth, that the number of the laborers and the measure of the harvest does actually depend upon their prayer."[87]

> The number of missionaries on the field is entirely dependent on someone praying out laborers.
> Andrew Murray

E. M. Bounds states, "The mightiest successes that come to God's cause are created and carried on by prayer in God's day of power. God shapes the world by prayer....God's conquering days are when the saints have given themselves to mightiest prayer."[88]

Evangelistic Praying

L. R. Scarborough said, "Prayer conditions power. Prayer makes possible power. And power is essential in winning men to Christ."[89]

Thomas Brooks wrote, "There is nothing that renders Satan's plots fruitless like prayer!"[90]

A. C. Dixon expressed prayer power thus: "When we depend upon our money, our teaching, our education, our preaching, we get what these can do….But when we depend upon prayer, we get what God can do."[91]

J. C. Ryle cites some wonderful examples in Scripture of the power of prayer: "Nothing seems to be too great, too hard, or too difficult for prayer to do. It has obtained things that seemed impossible and out of reach. It has won victories over fire, air, earth, and water. Prayer opened up the Red Sea. Prayer brought water from the rock and bread from Heaven. Prayer made the sun stand still. Prayer brought fire from the sky on Elijah's sacrifice. Prayer turned the counsel of Ahithophel into foolishness. Prayer overthrew the army of Sennacherib. Well might Mary, Queen of Scots say, 'I fear John Knox's prayers more than an army of ten thousand men.' Prayer has healed the sick. Prayer has raised the dead. Prayer has procured the conversion of souls."[92]

Prayer Is More Powerful Than Money

E. M. Bounds emphasized that foreign missions [and I add home missions] needs "more the power of prayer than the power of money."[93] He continues, "Prayer can make even poverty in the missionary cause move on amidst difficulties and hindrances. Much money without prayer is helpless and powerless in the face of the utter darkness and sin and wretchedness on the foreign field."[94] This does not in any wise dismiss the financial support laborers sorely need or that we should render. A. J. Dain states that the church at Antioch, in sending out Paul and Silas, "was prepared to forgo that which was normally permissible, be it food or leisure, in the high interest of the church's evangelistic outreach. The personal sacrifice of those two first intrepid missionaries was matched by the sacrifice, identification, and prayer of the church which sent them forth."[95]

Give financially to evangelistic causes and laborers, but saturate the gift in prayer prior to sending it to fulfill its mission. Recall that Jesus first blessed the loaves and the fishes (Matthew 14:15–21) prior to their distribution, which resulted in the miraculous feeding of five thousand people with twelve basketfuls left over. Praying over your gift prior to its dis-

Power

bursement empowers it to do the unthinkable, unexpected, and almost the unbelievable.

How might the believer possess such power in evangelistic praying? C. H. Spurgeon gives answer: "To sum it all up, if you want that splendid power in prayer, you must remain in loving, living, lasting, conscious, practical, abiding union with the Lord Jesus Christ; and if you get to that by divine grace, then you shall ask what you will, and it shall be done unto you"[96] (John 15:7). The power in evangelistic praying is linked to the sovereignty of God who is able to supply its answer.

Power

Chapter Six

Passion

Take those first steps in evangelism because you love God. It is not primarily out of compassion for humanity that we share our faith or pray for the lost; it is, first of all, love for God.[97] ~ John Piper

To stand before men on behalf of God is one thing. To stand before God on behalf of men is something entirely different.[98] ~ Leonard Ravenhill

The Lord wake us from this stonyhearted barbarity to our fellowmen and make us yearn over them, care about them, pray about them, and work for them till the Lord shall arise and send forth laborers into His harvest![99] ~ C. H. Spurgeon

We discover the passion necessary for evangelistic praying from the example of Jesus. Matthew says, "Jesus now travelled through all the towns and villages, teaching in their synagogues, proclaiming the Gospel of the kingdom, and healing all kinds of illness and disability. As he looked at the vast crowds he was deeply moved with pity for them, for they were as bewildered and miserable as a flock of sheep with no shepherd" (Matthew 9:35–36 Phillips).

It was Jesus' broken heart for the lost that moved Him to pray for them and for laborers to go to them. Jesus showed no favoritism. He showed compassion to the whole *multitude*. Elsewhere in Scripture the compassion of Jesus for souls was communicated by His touch (Mark 1:40–41), tears (Luke 19:41–44), teaching (Luke 15:20), talk (Luke 8:26–39; 23:34), and torture (Matthew 27:24–50; John 19:18).

Why don't we obey Jesus' instruction and cry out for more laborers in prayer? It's because of the absence of passionate love for Jesus. "Our passion for Christ," states Hyman J. Appelman, "will generate within us a compassion for the souls of men. The two are inseparable. They ever go together."[100] A passion for the lost flows from the heart of Christ into the heart of those who love Him "with all [their] heart, all [their] soul, all [their] strength, and all [their] mind" (Luke 10:27 NLT). Not until we truly have a "crazy love" for Jesus will a concern for the unsaved be manifested.

Evangelistic Praying

Through loving Jesus, the believer will view the lost through His lenses, which will lead to exhibiting evangelistic compassion by praying for them and for laborers to go to them.

Oswald J. Sanders bears this out in saying, "Oh, to realize that souls, precious, never-dying souls, are perishing all around us, going out into the blackness of darkness and despair, eternally lost; and yet to feel no anguish, shed no tears, know no travail! How little we know of the compassion of Jesus!"[101] General William Booth was notified by one of his captains that the work was so difficult that no progress had been made. Booth replied with two words: "Try tears." Success soon was known in the work.[102] "Oh, for the tears of Jesus," says Hyman J. Appelman. "Cry unto God, beloved. Cry unto God for the gift of passion, the gift of tears."[103] Oh, for the tears of Jesus to flow from our eyes for the eternally doomed as they are bathed in prayer.

Not only must evangelistic praying be compassionate, but also of fervent pitch (James 5:16). Prayer may be of the hot nature without being highly emotional. D. L. Moody, quoting Bishop Hall, emphasizes the need of fervency in prayer: "An arrow, if it be drawn up but a little way, goes not far; but if it be pulled up to the head, it flies swiftly and pierces deep. Thus prayer, if it be only dribbled forth from careless lips, falls at our feet. It is the strength of ejaculation and strong desire which sends it to Heaven and makes it pierce the clouds."[104]

> Prayer, if it be only dribbled forth from careless lips, falls at our feet.
> Bishop Hall

The Puritan Thomas Brooks said, "As a painted fire is no fire, a dead man no man, so a cold prayer is no prayer....Cold prayers are as arrows without heads, as swords without edges, as birds without wings: they pierce not, they cut not, they fly not up to Heaven. Cold prayers do always freeze before they reach to Heaven."[105] Brooks then challenged the believer: "Oh, that Christians would chide themselves out of their cold prayers and chide themselves into a better and warmer frame of spirit when they make their supplications to the Lord!"[106] And I say a hearty amen to that!

Chapter Seven

Pleading

The prayer warrior must learn how to plead the victory of Calvary, for the blood of the Lamb has forever broken the power of the Devil and robbed him of his prey. Plead the blood of the Lamb for the liberation of the soul for whom you pray.[107] ~ Oswald Sanders

Talking to men for God is a great thing, but talking to God for men is greater still. He will never talk well and with real success to men for God who has not learned well how to talk to God for men.[108] ~ E. M. Bounds

We should try to bear in our hearts the whole world, the heathen, the Jews, the body of true believers, the professing Protestant churches, the country in which we live, the congregation to which we belong, the household in which we sojourn, the friends and relations we are connected with. For each and all of these we should plead.[109] ~ J. C. Ryle

It is the aimlessness of prayer that accounts for so many seemingly unanswered prayers. Be specific in your petitions.[110] ~ Adam Clark

The believer is to pray for laborers to be supplied. Often this cuts against the grain. We prefer to form "think tanks," strategize, and form study committees to ascertain what might be done to place more laborers in the harvest. There is a willingness to do almost anything save the one thing Jesus says is the most needful, and that is to pray for workers to be thrust out into the harvest.

Only God can call forth the laborers. Therefore, prayers and petitions for them is not to be made of convention or denominational headquarters or anyone else but Him. Jesus clearly said that harvest helpers are not to be solicited by man but divinely summoned; not recruited "in," but prayed "out" through prayer. Why? John Gill, writing in his commentary, gives answer: "They could not make, qualify, and send out ministers themselves; this is not man's work, but God's: He only is able to furnish with ministerial gifts, to work upon and powerfully incline the hearts of men to this service, to call and send them forth into it, and to assist and succeed them in it."[111] The bottom line is that only Jesus can supply the kind of laborers needed, and when and where they are needed.

Evangelistic Praying

Jesus' command for us to pray for laborers is much stronger than simply "to pray." There are several Greek verbs that can be translated "pray." The one used in Matthew 9:38 is *deomai,* which means "to beseech, to plead earnestly, to beg" with urgency. The same word for prayer is used by the desperate father who sought the expulsion of demonic spirits from his son by Jesus (Luke 9:38) and by the leper who fell to the ground begging Jesus for healing (Luke 5:12). Jesus instructs the believer to pray, cry out to God for more laborers, with the tenacity of the leper and the father of the demon-possessed son.

The Greek verb *ekballo,* translated "send forth" (see also Luke 10:2), means "to drive or thrust forth," indicating the urgency of the mission, according to Vincent. The same verb is used for casting out demons (Matthew 8:16), and also when Jesus drove the moneychangers out of the temple (John 2:15). The same mighty power that it took to cast out demons and drive out the moneychangers is necessary for God to thrust laborers into the harvest, Jesus states. The verb alone (if there were nothing else) indicates the intensity required in praying for laborers to be dispatched.

Putting the two words (*deomai* and *ekballo*) together makes the point that you should pray as earnestly for laborers to be thrust out into the "harvest" as you would pray for a demon to be cast out of one who is possessed.

> Pray as earnestly for laborers to be thrust out into the harvest as you would pray for a demon to be cast out of one who is possessed.

The ripeness of the harvest dictates radical praying for laborers because the opportunity is temporary. "The harvest is past, the summer is ended, and we are not saved" (Jeremiah 8:20). Shortly the harvest (time for gathering the wheat into the barn) will be ended. "We must work the works of him who sent me while it is day; night is coming, when no one can work" (John 9:4 ESV). Dr. Samuel Johnson had engraved upon the dial of his watch: "The Night Cometh." May we have the words emblazoned upon the wall of our heart as a constant reminder of how little time remains to reap the harvest.

James said, "The insistent prayer of a righteous person is powerfully effective" (James 5:16 WEB). Pray urgently and persistently for laborers that the wheat might be gathered into the barn before it's eternally too late. James further states that the reason why so little is being accomplished in

Pleading

the harvest is due to the believers' failure to ask (James 4:2). How many laborers have not been provided simply because of the failure to ask God for them? How many souls yet remain in darkness, depravity and despair because of the failure of believers to knock on Heaven's door? How many doors yet remain closed to the Gospel because of our failure to storm God's throne seeking their opening? Sadly, James is right. We have not because we fail to ask.

During the Exodus, Moses invokes in prayer repeatedly "the name of the Lord" for the people's unbelief and disobedience. Pleading the name of the Lord in intercessory prayer for laborers and the lost is not an incantation but a reminder to God of who He has revealed Himself to be[112] and to us of His omnipotence "to do exceeding abundantly above all that we ask or think" (Ephesians 3:20) and that "whatever you ask in my name, that will I do" (John 14:13 NASB). Use that holy name in prayer and intercession.

Intercession for the Unsaved

After struggling with intercession for the lost for twenty years without success, a saint discovered the foundational key for effectual prayer—the basis of redemption. She surmises, "In reality, Christ's redemption purchased all mankind, so that we may say that each one is actually God's purchased possession, although he is still held by the enemy. We must, through the prayer of faith, claim and take for God in the name of the Lord Jesus that which is rightfully His. This can be done only on the basis of redemption. This is not meant to imply that because all persons have been purchased by God through redemption they are automatically saved. They must believe and receive the Gospel for themselves, but our intercession enables them to do this."[113]

So stand in the gap, earnestly and consistently pleading the precious blood of Jesus Christ to avail in the life of the multitudinous lost in our world and for the dispatching of laborers into the harvest (Ezekiel 22:30).

Pray for *Cultivation* prior to the witness, that the soil in the soul of the sinner may be broken up, seeded and prepared for the presentation of the Gospel (Hosea 10:12).

Pray for *Orchestration* of the witness, that the Holy Spirit will lead the right laborer to the person at the most opportune time to share the Gospel (Matthew 9:38).

Evangelistic Praying

Pray for *Reception* to the witness, that the sinner will be open to the presentation.

Pray for *Illumination* in the witness, that the Holy Spirit will open blinded eyes that divine truth may be revealed and received (Acts 26:18; Acts 16:14).

Pray for *Liberation* in the witness, that every satanic stronghold in the heart would be destroyed, resulting in total deliverance (Matthew 12:29).

Pray for *Conviction* in the witness, that the sinner will see his disobedience (failure to keep the Ten Commandments) toward God (John 16:8).

Pray for *Conversion* in the witness, that the lost person may express godly sorrow regarding his crime against God and in faith receive Jesus Christ as Lord and Savior (Acts 20:21).

Use Scripture Verses to Pray for the Unsaved

John 6:44
Father, I ask in Jesus' name that You would draw _____ to Yourself that he might believe and be saved.

2 Peter 3:9
Father, I thank You that it's not Your will that ____ die lost and experience eternal separation from You in Hell, but that he might be saved. Quicken him unto salvation today.

Matthew 13:1—9
Father, orchestrate circumstances in ____ life today that somehow by someone the Word may be sown in his heart and be met with receptivity.

Matthew 7:21
O Lord, ____ professes to know You but is deceived in this by Satan. Open his eyes to the truth of his soul's condition that he may acknowledge his lostness and be genuinely saved.

Ephesians 2:1
Lord Jesus, even as you quickened me when I was dead in trespasses and sins, please quicken ____ that he may know You as I do.

1 Timothy 1:15
Jesus, Your purpose in coming into the world was to save sinners.

Pleading

Please make this purpose known to ____, a sinner who stands in need of Your forgiveness and grace.

John 16:8
Holy Spirit, it is Your divine work on earth to convict lost man of his sin and need of salvation through Jesus Christ. Do this, Thy office work, in the heart of _____ today, I plead.

Isaiah 64:6
Heavenly Father, reveal to _____ that to trust in one's own goodness for salvation is futile. Help him understand that his best righteousness is but as a filthy rag in Your sight and that salvation is solely based on a relationship with You through your Son, Jesus Christ.

Romans 10:14
Lord Jesus, _____ needs to hear a clear presentation of the Gospel and then be given an opportunity to respond. Keep sending preachers, soul winners and Sunday school teachers to him until he hears, believes and calls upon Your name in faith and repentance to be saved.

Matthew 12:27–29
Father, I ask in Jesus' name that the strongman be bound in ____ life that he might believe and be set free.

Isaiah 35:5
Lord, under the preaching of the Word please open the blind eyes and deaf ears of ____ to the truth about sin, judgment and things to come that he might turn from sin unto Jesus Christ and be saved.

Chapter Eight

Profit

Now this is the confidence that we have in Him, that if we ask anything according to His will, He hears us. And if we know that He hears us, whatever we ask, we know that we have the petitions that we have asked of Him. ~ 1 John 5:14–15 NKJV

By intercessory prayer we can hold off Satan from other lives and give the Holy Ghost a chance with them. No wonder Jesus put such tremendous emphasis on prayer. ~ Oswald Chambers

Even as the moon influences the tides of the sea, even so does prayer influence the tides of godliness.[114] ~ C. H. Spurgeon

Every work of God can be traced to some kneeling form. ~ D. L. Moody

Referencing the profit of evangelistic praying, John MacArthur said that "the believers' prayers participate in the fulfillment of God's plans."[115]

Andrew Murray said, "How little Christians really feel and mourn the need of laborers in the fields of the world so white to the harvest. And how little they believe that our labor supply depends on prayer, that prayer will really provide "as many as he needeth."[116]

How is evangelistic praying profitable?

It Is Profitable Regarding Workers Being Sent Out

The implication is that the disciples, after praying for laborers as Jesus instructed (Matthew 9:38), were sent out two by two (Matthew 10:5–6; Mark 6:7) into the harvest.

Antioch Church and Paul
The Apostle Paul was sent out as a missionary as a result of the prayers of the leaders in the Antioch Church (Acts 13:2–6).

Peter and Cornelius
The Apostle Peter was sent to Cornelius in response to his (Cornelius') prayers (Acts 10:30–32).

Evangelistic Praying

Northfield Bible Conference

The famous Northfield Bible Conference in July 1886, where thousands of students responded to the call to be volunteer missionaries, was preceded by years of intercessory praying for laborers.

The Haystack Prayer Meeting

In 1806, a Williams College student named Samuel Mills began to pray for the cause of foreign missions. One August day he invited five others to join him in praying. It is said that as they prayed a thunderstorm developed, forcing them to shelter under a haystack. That day became the launch for a weekly prayer time known as the *Haystack Prayer Meeting*. In answer to their praying, God established the American Board of Commissioners of Foreign Missions, the American Bible Society, and the United Foreign Missionary Society from which the Lord sent many workers into His ripened harvest.

China

In 1949 Madame Chiang Kai-shek organized a prayer group to pray for someone to preach the Gospel in Taiwan to about a half-million Chinese Nationalist Army soldiers. They prayed, "Lord, haven't you got someone to gather the harvest?" Dick Hillis was one of three men who responded. Under his ministry, in just four months, five thousand of the soldiers were saved.

Africa

I heard the story of an elderly woman, a prayer warrior in California, who upon her deathbed heard that some places in Africa did not have a single Christian witness. One day she read the story of King Hezekiah (2 Kings 20:6) and prayed, "Lord, if you will add fifteen years to my life, I will pray laborers into those parts of Africa." The Lord heard the prayer, granting her extended years of life, and she in turn prayed laborers into those unevangelized parts of Africa. In fact, she lived to see such a great influx of missionaries into those regions that a missionary society recognized those places as her mission field.

My Call

You see the profit of such praying in me. Fifty or more years ago, a Christian somewhere prayed for God to raise up a vocational evangelist, and God "thrust" me into the work as a college student. Perhaps in Heaven I will be honored with the joy of meeting that person.

Profit

But the profit of such praying is equally visible in every church regarding those who serve as pastor, minister of music, pianist/organist, youth or children's minister, Sunday school teacher, and soul winner, among others.

In Matthew 8, a centurion approached Jesus for the healing of his dying servant. Jesus said to him, "Go thy way; and as thou hast believed, so be it done unto thee. And his servant was healed in the selfsame hour" (v. 13). David Wilkerson, commenting on this text, said, "I believe the same thing happens with all who intercede for the harvest. While we're asking God to send forth laborers, the Holy Spirit is stirring someone somewhere. The fact is, while we're praying, the Holy Spirit is searching the earth, putting an urgency in the hearts of those who desire to be used of the Lord. He's touching people everywhere, setting them apart for his service."[117]

It Is Profitable Regarding the Salvation of Souls

In response to evangelistic praying (where the Gospel seed has been sown), the lost are convicted of sin and their need of salvation. Prayer is the key that opens the eyes of those who are spiritually blind to their need of Jesus Christ. J. Sidlow Baxter said, "Men may spurn our appeals, reject our message, oppose our arguments, despise our persons, but they are helpless against our prayers."[118] Isaiah's words, "For as soon as Zion travailed, she brought forth her children" (Isaiah 66:8) serve as an instructive lesson to the saint regarding intercession for the unsaved, complete with promise. As a woman in giving birth to a child travails in pain and agony almost to the brink of death until her child is born, just so the believer is to exhibit spiritual birth pains in praying for the lost until they are born into God's wonderful family. The plain fact is that souls are saved when God's people pray.

"Not only can prayer reach Heaven," states Wesley Duwell, "but the arm of prayer can span the miles to any part of the world; and you in your place of intercession can touch someone who needs you, even thousands of miles away. This is not make-believe. It is spiritual reality."[119]

Jesus' prayer for the lost as He hung upon the cross (Luke 23:34) was answered in part on the Day of Pentecost when three thousand were saved (Acts 2:41), and continues to be answered as multitudes are saved. Stephen's prayer for the crowd who were stoning him to death (Acts 7:59–60) was answered in the eventual salvation of the Apostle Paul and

Evangelistic Praying

doubtless of others who witnessed the murder. George Müller prayed every day without exception for five men to be saved. The first was saved within eighteen months. The second was saved five years later. The third man was saved six years later. However, fifty-two years from the time he began praying for the five men, the other two were not saved despite his daily pleadings. Following Müller's death, his prayers were answered. They both were saved. God certainly honored the prayer of these men for the lost to be saved. Likewise, He will honor yours.

It Is Profitable Regarding Open Doors

In the popular film *The Sound of Music,* Maria von Trapp's character realized her plans for life were futile. To console herself she says, "When the Lord closes a door, somewhere He opens a window." And He does this in response to the prayers of His people.

Lydia's heart was opened by the Lord "to heed the things spoken by Paul" (Acts 16:14 NKJV) in response to prayer (Acts 16:13). In the same way He opens the door to nations, governments, and people groups for the proclamation of the Gospel. "The Holy One, the True One, the One who has the Key of David, who opens and no one will close, and closes and no one opens says: I know your works. Because you…have not denied My name, look, I have placed before you an open door that no one is able to close" (Revelation 3:7–8 HCSB). It is God's responsibility in response to prayer to open doors that none other can open so the Gospel may be proclaimed. And this He does. Paul, while imprisoned, requested the Colossian saints to pray for open doors of ministry that he might preach Christ (Colossians 4:3). Across the globe there are many Christian laborers who beg the same of you.

Don't Ram a Door Open.

John Stott comments, "Christ has the keys, and He opens the doors. Then let us not barge our way unceremoniously through doors which are still closed. We must wait for Him to make openings for us. Damage is continually being done to the cause of Christ by rude or blatant testimony. It is indeed right to seek to win for Christ our friends and relatives at home and at work, but we are sometimes in a greater hurry than God is. Be patient, pray hard, love much, and wait expectantly for the opportunity of witness. The same applies to our future. More mistakes are probably made by speed than by sloth, by impatience than by deleteriousness. God's purposes often ripen slowly, and if the door is shut, don't put your shoulder

Profit

to it. Wait till Christ takes out the key and opens it up."[120] I count every facet of my ministry as an "open door" from God. I pray the doors may remain open with others opening along the way.

It Is Profitable Regarding the Spirituality of the Saint

C. H. Spurgeon tags the primary reason for carnality in the saint as prayerlessness. He said, "Why is it that some Christians, although they hear many sermons, make but slow advances in the divine life? Because they neglect their closets."[121] One cannot pray evangelistically without having his heart inflamed for the Savior and the lost. Warren Wiersbe says, "It is *laborers*, not spectators, who pray for laborers."[122] You cannot remain on the sideline if you pray evangelistically. You will be compelled to be an answer to your own prayer, as the twelve disciples were, who I suggest took Matthew 9:38 to heart praying for laborers. E. M. Bounds speaks of the value of intercessory prayer to the believer: "Few things give such quickened and permanent vigor to the soul as a long, exhaustive season of importunate prayer. It gives a new life, a soldierly training, to religion."[123]

"Prayer has a way of molding us," state Fish and Conant, "so that God can use us as channels. God's power is Holy, and he cannot compromise his holiness by letting his power flow through an unclean channel."[124] E. M. Bounds writes, "Secret praying is the test, the gauge, the conserver of man's relation to God."[125] Jack Hyles says, "If we spend enough time praying for laborers, then we ourselves become better laborers. If we are required to look at the harvest fields and to plead with God to send laborers into those fields, we ourselves will have our burden for the work increased, which will be followed by a new zeal and dedication to the work."[126] Hyles continues, "We often become the answer to our prayer. As we become more burdened for the work because we pray for laborers, sometimes we become one of those laborers."[127]

> Secret praying is the test, the gauge, the conserver of man's relation to God.
> E. M. Bounds

Andrew Murray, in *The Ministry of Intercession,* wrote, "If we desire to be delivered from the sin of neglecting prayer, we must enlarge our hearts for the work of intercession. Praying constantly for ourselves will come to failure. Only in intercession for others will our faith, love, and

Evangelistic Praying

perseverance be aroused, and the power of the Spirit, which can fit us for saving men, be found."[128]

Praying for laborers also softens our hearts, making us more receptive to our children being chosen by the Lord to fill a ministry or mission gap at home or abroad.

> Give of thy sons to bear the message glorious;
>> Give of thy wealth to speed them on their way.
> Pour out thy soul for them in prayer victorious,
>> And all thou spendest Jesus will repay. ~ Mary A. Thompson

The happiest Christians are the obedient. Your cup will never overflow with satisfaction and jubilation to the degree it might, should evangelistic praying and going be neglected.

It Is Profitable Regarding Heaven's Joy and Ours

In the parable of the lost sheep, it is stated that when the shepherd found the lost sheep, "he layeth it on his shoulders, rejoicing. And when he cometh home, he calleth together his friends and neighbors, saying unto them, Rejoice with me; for I have found my sheep which was lost" (Luke 15:5–6). The bottom line for evangelistic praying is that the lost sheep (the spiritually dead) may be made alive in Christ Jesus. And upon this happening, *the saint experiences a joy* incomparable, unspeakable and full of glory. It's party time every time a soul is saved.

> There is joy on earth among the righteous,
>> Joy beyond compare,
> When a soul returns to Christ for shelter—
>> Finds forgiveness there. ~ Daniel O. Teasley, 1911

Dr. John MacArthur brings this truth home to our hearts in the sermon *Heaven's Joy Recovering the Lost.* He states, "We find our joy in this world in a lot of ways. But if you want to get in touch with God and you want to share the joy of Heaven, you're going to find your greatest joy in the salvation of the sinner, in the recovery of the lost."[129] Hyman Appelman agrees, saying that soul winning "outstrips and outweighs any and every other benediction and pleasure that comes to the human heart."[130]

Profit

Watchman Nee stated, "Beloved, there are two big days in the life of a believer: the day on which he believes in the Lord, and every day after that when he leads someone to faith in Christ."[131] All who have won a soul to Christ agree wholeheartedly. C. H. Spurgeon testifies of the believer's joy in bringing a lost soul to Jesus Christ. He says, "If you are eager for real joy, I am persuaded that no joy of growing wealthy, no joy of increasing knowledge, no joy of influence over your fellow creatures, no joy of any other sort can ever be compared with the rapture of saving a soul from death and helping to restore our lost brethren to our great Father's house."[132]

Though the believer may only play a *role* in bringing one soul to the Savior, he accomplishes far more than the preacher, teacher, singer or missionary who amidst the good they do win none. A Puritan writer has said, "God never gives any one man a whole soul." Soul winning is teamwork. The apostle explains, "What then is Apollos? And what is Paul? Servants through whom you believed, even as the Lord gave opportunity to each one. I planted, Apollos watered, but God was causing the growth. So then neither the one who plants nor the one who waters is anything, but God who causes the growth. Now he who plants and he who waters are one; but each will receive his own reward according to his own labor. For we are God's fellow workers; you are God's field, God's building" (1 Corinthians 3:5–9 NASB).

We must be ready to sow and allow another to reap and equally ready to reap the harvest wherein we did not sow, all the while giving God the glory and honor (John 3:30). In this we are partakers in His joy.

But not only is such praying *profitable regarding the joy of the saint, but also of Heaven.* In the aforementioned parable, Jesus continued by saying, "I say unto you, that likewise joy shall be in heaven over one sinner that repenteth, more than over ninety and nine just persons, which need no repentance" (Luke 15:7). What brings ecstatic joy to God, the angels and the redeemed saints in Heaven is news that a lost soul has been saved. Again, Spurgeon remarks, "It is a bliss above bliss—a joy that rises out of joy like some huge Atlantic billow that towers above all the rest of the waves. They have a special, extra, doubly distilled joy in Heaven sometimes, and that comes to them whenever one sinner repents!"[133] Bailey Smith states, "Evangelism makes Heaven happy because it is the only hope—absolutely the only hope for sinful man."[134]

Evangelistic Praying

There is joy, glad joy among the angels,
    Joy in Heav'n above,
When a soul returns from sin and folly
    To the Savior's love.

There is joy, more joy among the angels,
    When the lost is found,
Than for nine and ninety of the righteous
    Who in grace abound.

Joy among the angels,
Joy in heav'n above,
Joy on earth among the righteous
When the wanderer returns to the fold. ~ Daniel O. Teasley, 1911

Bring Joy to the Heart of God

What might the believer do to bring added pleasure and joy to our beloved Savior? Jesus says he can do so by leading a sinner to repent and trust Him as Lord and Savior. Just think, you and I in winning a soul can cause Jesus' heart to rejoice with great delight. The happiest days in Heaven are the ones in which a sinner repents and is wondrously saved, which our praying and soul winning produce.

> The man who truly prays gets from God many
> things denied to the prayerless man.
> E. M. Bounds

E. M. Bounds said, "The man who truly prays gets from God many things denied to the prayerless man."[135] To him prayer is wondrously profitable, personally and to others corporately.

Chapter Nine

Persistency

One day Jesus told his disciples a story to show that they should always pray and never give up. ~ Luke 18:1 NLT

The enemy will use every possible means to silence our intercession and to block our attack against him.[136] ~ Unknown

The great fault of the children of God is, they do not continue in prayer; *they do not go on praying; they do not persevere.* If they desire anything for God's glory, they should pray until they get it.[137] ~ George Müller

Let us, when we pray for His church or any portion of it, under the power of the world, asking Him to visit her with the mighty workings of His Spirit and to prepare her for His coming, let us pray in the assured faith: prayer does help; praying always and not fainting will bring the answer. Only give God time. And then keep crying day and night. 'Hear what the unrighteous judge saith. And shall not God avenge His own elect, which cry to Him day and night, and He is long-suffering over them. I say unto you, He will avenge them speedily.'[138] ~ Andrew Murray

A favorite verse of John "Praying" Hyde of India was:

I have set watchmen on your walls, O Jerusalem;
They shall never hold their peace day or night.
You who make mention of the LORD, do not keep silent,
And give Him no rest till He establishes
And till He makes Jerusalem a praise in the earth (Isaiah 62:6–7 NKJV).

Hyde believed he was such a watchman and made intercession for laborers and the unsaved day and night. He died at the age of 47 from the effects of his intense and persistent intercession without food or sleep.[139]

Evangelistic Praying

Every believer is to be such a watchman making intercession for laborers and the souls of lost humanity continuously. Recall that it was the persistency in praying by Abraham that stayed judgment from Sodom and Gomorrah (Genesis 18:16–32). It was only when the praying ceased that God's wrath was poured out upon the city (Genesis 18:33). Our persistent intercession for people and countries may be staying God's hand of judgment from them. So pray on, dear saint; pray on until such time as laborers are provided among all peoples and nations of the world and all the world embraces Jesus Christ as Lord and Savior.

In Luke 11:5–10, Jesus gives a parable of the model of intercession. It is one of insistence and persistence. "Then, teaching them more about prayer, he used this story: 'Suppose you went to a friend's house at midnight, wanting to borrow three loaves of bread. You say to him, "A friend of mine has just arrived for a visit, and I have nothing for him to eat." And suppose he calls out from his bedroom, "Don't bother me. The door is locked for the night, and my family and I are all in bed. I can't help you." But I tell you this—though he won't do it for friendship's sake, if you keep knocking long enough, he will get up and give you whatever you need because of your shameless persistence. And so I tell you, keep on asking, and you will receive what you ask for. Keep on seeking, and you will find. Keep on knocking, and the door will be opened to you. For everyone who asks, receives. Everyone who seeks, finds. And to everyone who knocks, the door will be opened'" (NLT).

"Without persistence," E. M. Bounds cautions, "prayers may go unanswered. Importunity is made up of the ability to hold on, to continue, to wait with unrelaxed and unrelaxable grasp, restless desire, and restful patience. Importunate prayer… is not an option but a necessity."[140] Bounds continues by warning against hurried praying: "I think Christians fail so often to get answers to their prayers because they do not wait long enough on God. They just drop down and say a few words and then jump up and forget it and expect God to answer them. Such praying always reminds me of the small boy ringing his neighbor's doorbell and then running away as fast as he can go."[141]

S. D. Gordon reminds the believer of Satan's stranglehold on the unsaved, necessitating persevering and persistent prayer for their release. He states, "The enemy yields only what he must. He yields only what is taken. Therefore, the ground must be taken step by step. Prayer must be definite. He yields only when he must. Therefore, the prayer must be per-

Persistency

sistent. He continually renews his attacks; therefore, the ground taken must be *held* against him in the Victor's name."[142]

How long should I pray evangelistically for laborers or souls? "'Shouldn't I come to the place where I stop praying and leave the matter in God's hands?' The only answer is this: *Pray until what you are praying for is accomplished or until you have complete assurance in your heart it will be....*

"In the first instance, we stop because we actually see the answer. In the second, we stop because we believe, and faith in our hearts is as trustworthy as the sight of our eyes, for it is, 'faith, *from* God' (Ephesians 6:23) and the 'faith *of* God' (Romans 3:3) that we have within us."[143] How long we should pray is answered also by John Bradford. He says, "When I know what I want, I always stop and continue to present that prayer until I feel that I have pleaded it with God and until God and I have had dealings with each other upon it. I never go on to another petition until I have completely gone through the first."[144]

An anonymous writer said, "The one concern of the Devil is to keep us from praying. He fears nothing from prayerless studies, prayerless work and religion. He laughs at our toil, mocks our wisdom, but he trembles when we pray." So having prayed, pray.

Chapter Ten

Practice

In the morning will I direct my prayer unto thee, and will look up. ~ Psalm 5:3

We all struggle and fumble along, for prayer is both the highest and most difficult of all spiritual practices. But God will help us if we just give Him a chance.[145] ~ Jim Cymbala

It is useless to say you know not how to pray. Prayer is the simplest act in all religion. It is simply speaking to God. It needs neither learning nor wisdom nor book-knowledge to begin it. It needs nothing but heart and will.[146] ~ J. C. Ryle

Though your words are broken and your sentences disconnected, God will hear you.[147] ~ C. H. Spurgeon

We need the presence and the power of God that comes to those who wait upon Him in prayer.[148] ~ W. A. Criswell

You can do more than pray *after* you have prayed, but you can never do more than pray *until* you have prayed.[149] ~ A. J. Gordon

One is staggered at the unwillingness of Christians to pray. Perhaps it is because they have never experienced, or even heard of, convincing answers to prayer.[150] ~ Unknown

Jesus Christ carries on intercession *for* us in Heaven; the Holy Ghost carries on intercession *in* us on earth; and we, the saints, have to carry on intercession for all men.[151] ~ Oswald Chambers

The Apostle Paul exhorts us to devote ourselves to prayer (Colossians 4:2) and to pray without ceasing (1 Thessalonians 5:17). G. K. Chesterton did both. Once he remarked, "You say grace before meals. All right. But I say grace before the concert and the opera; and grace before the play and pantomime; and grace before I open a book; and grace before sketching, painting, swimming, fencing, boxing, walking, playing, dancing; and grace before I dip the pen in the ink."[152] In essence he was saying that he prayed for and over all things in his life, seeking God's guidance, protection, empowerment and provision. Might we imitate him for our good and God's glory!

According to *LifeWay Research,* the five most prominent things for which people pray are family and friends (82 percent), personal problems (74 percent), good things that recently unfolded (54 percent), personal sin (42 percent), and people facing natural disasters (38 percent).[153] While such praying certainly is biblical and needful, Jesus implores us to include evangelistic praying (Matthew 9:38; Luke 10:2); in fact, He urges that intercession for laborers and the lost not be at the bottom of our prayer list, but at its top.

How to Pray

There is the danger of praying with form but without freedom, in which you stifle the delight of prayer and steal the power of prayer. This is not to discount the value in structured praying but to serve as merely a caution that such does not negate freedom in praying. God intends for intercession to be easy, enjoyable and heartfelt (not mechanical, ritualistic, boring and heartless). So don't feel guilty if you don't pray three hours a day as Dr. So-and-so advocates.

C. H. Spurgeon expounds my point: "Fluency is a questionable endowment, especially when it is not attended with weight of thought and depth of feeling. Some brethren pray by the yard, but true prayer is measured by weight and not by length. A single groan before God may have more fullness of prayer in it than a fine oration of great length."[154]

> God intends for intercession to be easy, enjoyable and heartfelt (not mechanical, ritualistic, boring and heartless). And it is, to the experienced intercessor.

Pray Aloud

Cry out to God in your closet, but also in public prayer meetings, for laborers and the lost (Psalm 27:7). Shrink not back. "The first hesitating, stumbling, ungrammatical prayer of a confused Christian," states Lyman Beecher, "may be worth more to the church than the best prayer of the most eloquent pastor."[155] C. H. Spurgeon said, "The cries of the lambs must mingle with the bleating of the sheep, or the flock will lack much of its natural music."[156] We learn to pray aloud by praying aloud.

Practice

The Old-Fashioned Prayer Meeting

It is with great delight that I recall Wednesday night prayer meeting in the student pastorates I served. In those days of old—get this—we actually prayed! Oh, for a return to such prayer meetings! Leonard Ravenhill said, "The Cinderella of the church of today is the prayer meeting. This handmaid of the Lord is unloved and unwooed. The prayer meeting is dead or dying."[157]

Jim Cymbala agrees. He says, "We teach about prayer; we sell books on prayer; and ministers extol the 'power of prayer.' We have prayer symposiums and seminars, a well-publicized 'National Day of Prayer' observance, even prayer manuals with all the relevant Scriptures clearly outlined. But the sad fact is that in both 'super' churches and smaller churches alike, the prayer meeting has almost become extinct! We do everything together but pray!"[158]

> Either initiate or join a weekly prayer group (it need
> not consist of many) that is both a "birth chamber"
> for the unsaved and "dispatch station" for laborers.

"There should be a birth chamber," writes Leonard Ravenhill, "in every church; [it] should be a room for travail."[159] Either initiate or join a weekly prayer group (it need not consist of many) that is both a "birth chamber" for the unsaved and "dispatch station" for laborers.

Jerry Rankin writes, "Just as churches adopt missionaries and pray for them, churches and individuals can adopt the people group with whom missionaries are working or an unreached group that is yet to be engaged with the Gospel. Testimonies are abundant of an evangelistic breakthrough after a people group has become the focus of a church's prayer."[160]

Sweet hour of prayer! sweet hour of prayer!
That calls me from a world of care
And bids me at my Father's throne
Make all my wants and wishes known.

In seasons of distress and grief,
My soul has often found relief
And oft escaped the tempter's snare
By thy return, sweet hour of prayer! ~ William W. Walford

Evangelistic Praying

In *Only a Prayer Meeting,* C. H. Spurgeon states, "Brethren, we shall never see much change for the better in our churches in general till the prayer meeting occupies a higher place in the esteem of Christians. To mix it up with a weeknight lecture, and really make an end of it, is a sad sign of declension. I wonder some two or three earnest souls in such churches do not band themselves together to restore the meeting for prayer and bind themselves with a pledge to keep it up whether the minister will come to it or not."[161]

Why not initiate the return of the old-fashioned prayer meeting at your church with focus upon praying for laborers and the lost? Yes, there is the risk of opposition, rebuke, and little interest in its return (Satan opposes the church on her knees more than anything else), but God will be highly pleased and the church greatly blessed with its engagement.

Answer Your Own Prayer

As you pray, remain available to be the laborer for whom you pray. "These same persons who are commanded to pray [for laborers] are presently appointed laborers themselves."[162] Corrie ten Boom underscores this element of prayer in saying, "We never know how God will answer our prayers, but we can expect that He will get us involved in His plan for the answer. If we are true intercessors, we must be ready to take part in God's work on behalf of the people for whom we pray."[163] David Wilkerson stated, "As laborers, we are the harvest instruments in the Lord's hand."[164]

> As laborers, we are the harvest instruments in the Lord's hand.
> David Wilkerson

God's Choice Instrument for the Harvest

But to be a laborer, anticipate refinement by the Lord. In the time of Jesus, men used a long curved single-edged blade with a handle (scythe) to harvest the crop. The instrument was forged by a blacksmith, who placed it into the fire and then upon the anvil to pound it into shape. The process was repeated until the blade was good and sharp. As God's scythe (instrument) to harvest the lost, a divine *pounding and forging* must be experienced to fashion us into powerful and effectual servants. Some instruments may need the process repeated several times for preparation for an intense and/or dangerous assignment.

Practice

The Potter's Wheel

The same idea is pictured in Jeremiah where God likens us to pots and Himself to the master Potter. In seeing flaws in the pots (the believer), He places them back onto the wheel to shape them into useable vessels and then into the furnace to *stablish* them in place (Jeremiah 18:1–6). Warren Wiersbe vividly describes the process. "The potter sat before two parallel stone wheels that were joined by a shaft. He turned the bottom wheel with his feet and worked the clay on the top wheel as the wheel turned."[165] The hard lump (resistance) in the clay has to be kneaded out for it to be pleasing and useful to the potter.

Paul uses the same simile: "Hath not the potter power over the clay, of the same lump to make one vessel unto honor, and another unto dishonor?" (Romans 9:21). Changing the figure somewhat, He wrote to Timothy: "If a man therefore purge himself from these, he shall be a vessel unto honor, sanctified, and meet for the master's use, and prepared unto every good work" (2 Timothy 2:21).

Shame in Time of Harvest

Failure to pray for laborers and the lost and failure to engage in soul winning in the time of harvest cause shame (Proverbs 10:5). R. G. Lee explains why. "Because the harvest will not wait. Harvest time is a crisis time. This crisis must be vigorously and promptly met. Grain, once ripe, must be gathered in at once, or it will fall to the ground and be lost....Doors once opened but unentered may close again. Minds made susceptible but not won to Christ may turn away and become hardened. Truth resisted once is easier to resist the next time, you know. We must strike while the iron is hot. It is now or never when the harvest is ripe and ready for reaping. Is the harvest song in our hearts, and are the harvest blades in our hands while the fields are 'white already to harvest'? 'Awake, thou that sleepest'!"[166]

A Puritan's Prayer for Laborers and the Lost

Sovereign God, Thy cause, not mine own, engages my heart; and I appeal to Thee with greatest freedom to set up Thy kingdom in every place where Satan reigns. Glorify Thyself and I shall rejoice, for to bring honor to Thy name is my sole desire. I adore Thee that Thou art God and long that others should know it, feel it, and rejoice in it. Oh, that all men might love and praise Thee, that Thou mightiest have all glory! Let sinners be

Evangelistic Praying

brought to Thee for Thy dear name! To the eye of reason everything respecting the conversion of others is as dark as midnight, but Thou canst accomplish great things. The cause is Thine, and it is to Thy glory that men should be saved. Lord, use me as Thou wilt, do with me what Thou wilt, but, oh, promote Thy cause; let Thy kingdom come; let Thy blessed interest be advanced in the world! Oh, do Thou bring great numbers to Jesus! Let me see that glorious day, and give me to grasp for multitudes of souls; let me be willing to die to that end; and while I live, let me labor for Thee to the utmost of my strength, spending time profitably in this work, both in health and in weakness. It is Thy cause and kingdom I long for, not mine own. Oh, answer Thou my request![167]

Have you requisitioned Heaven lately for necessary workers in your church, community, our country and around the world? Do you intercede in behalf of the lost all around you? Are you willing to be "thrust" into the mission field at your doorstep or around the world in answer to your own praying and God's calling?

9:38 Challenge

I challenge you to make a commitment to pray as instructed by our Lord, for laborers and the lost. Set the alarm on your watch or cell phone to ring at 9:38 a.m. daily to prompt prayer for laborers (Matthew 9:38). Let us be faithful in praying for laborers and the lost personally and corporately.

Pray out laborers into the nations of the world while there is yet time.

Afghanistan	Albania	Algeria
Andorra	Angola	Antigua and Barbuda
Argentina	Armenia	Aruba
Australia	Austria	Azerbaijan
Bahamas	Bahrain	Bangladesh
Barbados	Belarus	Belgium
Belize	Benin	Bhutan
Bolivia	Bosnia and Herzegovina	Botswana
Brazil	Brunei	Bulgaria
Burkina Faso	Burundi	Cambodia
Cameroon	Canada	Cape Verde

Practice

Central African Republic	Chad	Chile
China	Colombia	Comoros
Congo	Costa Rica	Cote d'Ivoire
Croatia	Cuba	Curacao
Cyprus	Czech Republic	Denmark
Djibouti	Dominica	Dominican Republic
DR Congo	Ecuador	Egypt
El Salvador	England	Equatorial Guinea
Eritrea	Estonia	Ethiopia
Fiji	Finland	France
French Guiana	Gabon	Gambia
Gaza Strip and West Bank	Georgia	Germany
Ghana	Greece	Greenland
Grenada	Guatemala	Guinea
Guinea-Bissau	Guyana	Haiti
Honduras	Hong Kong	Hungary
Iceland	India	Indonesia
Iran	Iraq	Ireland
Israel	Italy	Jamaica
Japan	Jordan	Kazakhstan
Kenya	Kiribati	Kosovo
Kuwait	Kyrgyzstan	Laos
Latvia	Lebanon	Lesotho
Liberia	Libya	Liechtenstein
Lithuania	Luxembourg	Macau
Macedonia	Madagascar	Malawi
Malaysia	Maldives	Mali
Malta	Marshall Islands	Mauritania
Mauritius	Mexico	Micronesia
Moldova	Monaco	Mongolia
Montenegro	Morocco	Mozambique
Myanmar (Burma)	Namibia	Nauru
Nepal	Netherlands	New Zealand
Nicaragua	Niger	Nigeria
North Korea	Northern Ireland	Norway
Oman	Pakistan	Palau

Evangelistic Praying

Panama	Papua New Guinea	Paraguay
Peru	Philippines	Poland
Portugal	Qatar	Romania
Russia	Rwanda	Saint Kitts and Nevis
Saint Lucia	Saint Vincent and the Grenadines	Samoa
San Marino	Sao Tome and Principe	Saudi Arabia
Scotland	Senegal	Serbia
Seychelles	Sierra Leone	Singapore
Saint Maarten	Slovakia	Slovenia
Solomon Islands	Somalia	South Africa
South Korea	South Sudan	Spain
Sri Lanka	Sudan	Suriname
Swaziland	Sweden	Switzerland
Syria	Taiwan	Tajikistan
Tanzania	Thailand	Timor-Leste
Togo	Tonga	Trinidad & Tobago
Tunisia	Turkey	Turkmenistan
Tuvalu	Uganda	Ukraine
Uruguay	United Arab Emirates	United States
Uzbekistan	Vanuatu	Venezuela
Vietnam	Wales	Western Sahara
Yemen	Zambia	Zimbabwe

Dr. Alexander Duff, the valiant veteran missionary to India, returned home (Scotland) to die. In giving a final appeal for laborers before the General Assembly of the Presbyterian Church, he fainted and was carried off the platform. As a doctor examined him, Duff opened his eyes.

"Where am I?" he cried. "Where am I?"

"Lie still," said the doctor. "Your heart is very weak."

"But," exclaimed the old warrior, "I must finish my appeal. Take me back. Take me back. I haven't finished my appeal yet."

"Lie still," said the doctor again, "You are too weak to go back."

But with determination, the aged saint struggled to his feet. With the

Practice

doctor on his one side and the moderator on the other, the old, white-haired warrior mounted the platform. He then continued his appeal.

"When Queen Victoria calls for volunteers for India," he exclaimed, "hundreds of young men respond; but when King Jesus calls, no one goes." Then he paused. Again he spoke. "Is it true," he asked, "that Scotland has no more sons to give for India?" Again he paused. "Very well," he concluded, "if Scotland has no more young men to send to India, then, old and decrepit though I am, I will go back, and even though I cannot preach, I can lie down on the shores of the Ganges and die in order to let the peoples of India know that there is at least one man in Scotland who cares enough for their souls to give his life for them."

Instantly young men from all over the assembly sprang to their feet crying out, "I'll go! I'll go! I'll go!" And many did go to India, investing their lives as missionaries as a result of the appeal God had made through His choicest servant Alexander Duff.

Pray for laborers, yes. But it cannot substitute for obedience to the call to be a laborer to the untold multitudes. In hearing the call (short-term or vocational), respond with the words of Isaiah, "Here am I; send me."

Chapter Eleven

Pledge

If there be any one point in which the Christian church ought to keep its fervor at a white heat, it is concerning missions. If there be anything about which we cannot tolerate lukewarmness, it is the matter of sending the gospel to a dying world.[168] ~ C. H. Spurgeon

In 1792, William Carey challenged his brethren to obey their responsibility to take the Gospel to unreached lands. *The Particular Baptist Society for Propagating the Gospel among the Heathen* was formed. At its meeting, Andrew Fuller remarked, "There is a gold mine in India, but it seems as deep as the center of the earth. Who will venture to explore it?"

An answer came from Carey, "I will venture to go down, but remember you must hold the ropes."

Fuller afterward said, "We solemnly engaged to do so, pledging ourselves never to desert him as long as we should live." William Carey spent forty years in India and translated the Bible into forty languages.

> Pledge yourself to personally hold the ropes for as many laborers in the harvest as possible (home and foreign) and communicate that commitment to them.

The need is drastic for more people to "hold the ropes" for missionaries, evangelists, translators and church planters. Though you may not be able to go to the "regions beyond" with the Gospel, you can facilitate that undertaking of others. Many yet would go, as Carey did, if they but knew someone would "hold the ropes."

In a fishing village that was located at the mouth of a turbulent river, a scream was heard: "Boy overboard!"

The strongest swimmer in the village tied a rope around his waist, threw the other among the crowd gathered, and plunged into the river. He gallantly fought the tide until he reached the young boy, and a great cheer

Evangelistic Praying

went up when he grasped him into his arms. He then shouted, "Pull in the rope!"

Each one on the shore looked one to the other, inquiring, "Who is holding the rope?" Sadly, no one was. In the excitement of watching the rescue effort, they had let the rope slip into the water. Unable to help, they watched two lives drown because no one made it his business to hold the end of the rope.

As God's chosen servants seek to rescue the unsaved locally and globally, make it your business to hold the shore end of the rope for them through intercessory prayer, encouragement and financial support. Pledge yourself to personally hold the ropes for as many laborers in the harvest as possible (home and foreign) and communicate that commitment to them.

Ekballo

E. M. Bounds reminds us that "prayers outlive the lives of those who uttered them. Outlive a generation; outlive an age; outlive a world."[169] To know the prayers put in motion today will yet be working until Jesus returns certainly should motivate us to pray more for laborers and the lost. Prayers unanswered in our lifetime will yet be at work afterward.

Therefore, continuously pray this: *Ekballo*! "Thrust forth laborers!"

Endnotes

[1] Oswald Chambers. *My Utmost for His Highest.* (Grand Rapids: Discovery House, 1992), June 20.

[2] L. B. Cowman. *Streams in the Desert.* (Grand Rapids: Zondervan, 2016), June 6.

[3] http://davidwilkersontoday.blogspot.com/2008/08/pray-lord-of-harvest.html, accessed June 20, 2017.

[4] C. H. Spurgeon. *The Power of Prayer in the Believer's Life.* (Lynwood, Washington: Emerald Books, 1993), 15.

[5] http://www.ccel.org/ccel/unknown/kneeling.vi.html, accessed May 5, 2017.

[6] J. C. Ryle. "A Call to Prayer," www.gracegems.org, accessed May 9, 2017.

[7] William Carver. *The Bible a Missionary Message.* (New York: Revell, 1921), 13.

[8] C. H. Spurgeon. *Metropolitan Tabernacle Pulpit,* Sermon #1127.

[9] Andrew Murray. *With Christ in the School of Prayer.* (Peabody, Massachusetts: Hendrickson Publishers, 2007), 53.

[10] George Sweeting. *How to Begin the Christian Life: Following Jesus as a New Believer.* (Chicago: Moody Publishers, 2012), Chapter 5.

[11] https://djameskennedy.org/devotional-detail/20150225-a-checklist-for-your-prayer-life, accessed May 9, 2017.

[12] E. M. Bounds. *The Purpose of Prayer.* (CreateSpace Independent Publishing Platform, April 1, 2014), Chapter 1.

[13] Ibid., 123.

[14] John Stott. *The Letters of John.* Tyndale New Testament Commentaries, rev. ed. (Leicester: IVP, 1988), 188.

[15] A. T. Pierson. *Forward Movements of the Last Half Century.* (New York & London: Funk & Wagnalls Company, 1900), 67.

[16] C. H. Spurgeon. "Prayer—The Forerunner of Mercy." Sermon #138, June 28, 1857.

[17] Chuck Swindoll. "Strengthening Your Grip on Prayer," March 18, 2014. https://www.insight.org/resources/article-library/individual/strengthening-your-grip-on-prayer, accessed May 24, 2017.

[18] Matthew Henry. *The Miscellaneous Works of the Rev. Matthew Henry.* (London: Joseph Ogle Robinson, 1833), 433.

[19] George Sweeting. *How to Begin the Christian Life: Following Jesus as a New Believer.* (Chicago: Moody Publishers, 2012), Chapter 5.

[20] Thomas Brooks. *The Privy View of Heaven, or Twenty Arguments for Closet Prayer.* (London: R. Pugh, 1820), 24.

[21] Ibid.

[22] C. H. Spurgeon. *Lectures to My Students.* (Grand Rapids: Zondervan Publishing House, 1970), 55.

[23] Ibid., 55–56.

[24] Ibid., p. 57.

[25] Ibid., p. 61.

[26] John Gill. *Exposition of the Entire Bible by John Gill.* (1763).

[27] J. C. Ryle. "A Call to Prayer," www.gracegems.org, accessed May 9, 2017.

Endnotes

[28] Andrew Murray. *With Christ in the School of Prayer.* (Peabody, Massachusetts: Hendrickson Publishers, 2007), 56.

[29] https://www.brainyquote.com/quotes/keywords/prayer.html, accessed May 26, 2017.

[30] Bailey Smith. *Real Evangelism.* (Nashville: Broadman Press, 1978), 84.

[31] John MacArthur. *Practical Wisdom for Pastors: Words of Encouragement and Counsel for a Lifetime of Ministry.* (Wheaton, IL: Crossway Books, 2001), Foreword.

[32] M. A. Darroch. *How Shall They Hear?* (Grand Rapids: Zondervan Publishing House, 1958), 39.

[33] E. M. Bounds. *The Essentials of Prayer: Prayer and Missions.* (Dallas: Gideon House Books, 2016), Chapter 13.

[34] American Baptist Missionary Union. *The Baptist Missionary Magazine*, Vol. 27. (Boston: John Putnam, 1847).

[35] John R. Rice. *The Evangelist.* (Murfreesboro: Sword of the Lord Publishers, 1968), 217.

[36] Matthew Poole. *Matthew Poole Commentary.* Matthew 9:37–38.

[37] Bailey Smith. *Real Evangelism.* (Nashville: Broadman Press, 1978), 85.

[38] Ibid. 84

[39] Robert E. Coleman. *The Master Plan of Evangelism.* (Grand Rapids: Revell, 1993), 94.

[40] C. H. Spurgeon. "The Whole Machinery of Salvation," a sermon preached August 18, 1889. http://www.spurgeon.org, accessed December 17, 2013.

[41] Jack Hyles. *Exploring Prayer with Jack Hyles: Praying for Laborers.* (Hammond, IN: Hyles-Anderson Publishers; 1983), Chapter 35.

[42] *Metropolitan Tabernacle Pulpit,* Sermon #1127.

[43] John Gill. *The New John Gill Exposition of the Entire Bible,* Commentary on Matthew 9:38. http://www.studylight.org/commentaries/geb/matthew-9.html. 1999. Bracket added by the author.

[44] M. A. Darroch. *How Shall They Hear?* (Grand Rapids: Zondervan Publishing House, 1958), 111.

[45] John MacArthur. "Do You Pray for the Lost?" August 18, 2016. https://www.gty.org/library/questions/QA060/do-you-pray-for-the-lost, accessed April 27, 2017.

[46] Robert G. Lee. *Sermonic Library: Seven Swords.* (Orlando, FL: Christ for the World Publishers, 1981), 53.

[47] Cited in Peter Lord. *The 29:59 Plan.* (Titusville, FL: Agape Ministries, 1976), 28.

[48] John MacArthur. *Alone with God.* (Colorado Springs: David C. Cook, 2011), 172.

[49] George W. Truett. *We Would See Jesus.* (Chattanooga: AMG Publishers, 1998), 87–88.

[50] Cited in John R. Rice. *The Soul Winner's Fire.* (Murfreesboro: Sword of the Lord, 1941), 117.

[51] Curtis Hutson, Ed. *Great Preaching on Prayer.* (Murfreesboro: Sword of the Lord, 1988), 13.

[52] David Wilkerson, *Bring Your Loved Ones to Christ.* (New Jersey: Fleming Revell Company, 1979), 116–117.

Endnotes

[53] Roy J. Fish and J. E. Conant. *Every Member Evangelism for Today.* (Harper & Row Publishers, 1976), 62. Cited in Bailey Smith, *Real Evangelism,* 83.

[54] http://davidwilkersontoday.blogspot.com/2010/03/pray-lord-of-harvest.html, accessed June 24, 2017.

[55] E. M. Bounds. *The Works of E. M. Bounds,* 196.

[56] Matthew Henry. *Matthew Henry's Commentary on the Whole Bible: Complete and Unabridged in One Volume.* (Peabody: Hendrickson, 1994), 2420.

[57] http://www.gospeltruth.net/ravenhill.htm, accessed May 30, 2017.

[58] J. C. Ryle. "A Call to Prayer," www.gracegems.org, accessed May 9, 2017.

[59] C. H. Spurgeon. "The Secret of Power in Prayer" (sermon #2002), http://www.spurgeongems.org/vols34-36/chs2002.pdf, accessed July 3, 2017.

[60] *China's Millions.* (Germantown, Philadelphia, PA: China Inland Mission, 1905), 115.

[61] Ibid.

[62] W. A. Criswell. "Power in Prayer" (Sermon), https://www.wacriswell.com/sermons/1967/power-in-prayer/, accessed May 16, 2017.

[63] George Sweeting. *How to Begin the Christian Life: Following Jesus as a New Believer.* (Chicago: Moody Publishers, 2012), Chapter 5.

[64] Curtis Hutson, Ed. *Great Preaching on Prayer.* (Murfreesboro: Sword of the Lord, 1988), 112.

[65] Andrew Murray. *The Ministry of Intercession.*

[66] Robert G. Lee. *Sermonic Library: Seven Swords.* (Orlando, FL: Christ for the World Publishers, 1981), 53.

[67] http://www.azquotes.com/quote/544952, accessed November 18, 2017.

[68] http://www.goodreads.com/quotes/tag/prayer?page=3, accessed May 23, 2017.

[69] Andrew Murray. *With Christ in the School of Prayer.* (Peabody, Massachusetts: Hendrickson Publishers, 2007), Ninth Lesson.

[70] J. C. Ryle. "A Call to Prayer," www.gracegems.org, accessed May 9, 2017.

[71] http://www.peoplegroups.org, accessed September 25, 2017. IMB updated figures as of September 24, 2017.

[72] Ibid.

[73] IMB. Lesson 1: Unreached and Unengaged People Groups, www.imb.org/ topic/explore-missions/missions-and-world-today/lesson-1-unreached-and-unengaged-people-groups, accessed September 25, 2017.

[74] Ibid.

[75] http://www.aboutmissions.org/top10.html (data could be up to ten years old), accessed June 22, 2017.

[76] The 10/40 Window: Getting to the Core of the Core. http://www.ad2000.org/1040broc.htm, accessed September 26, 2017.

[77] Mission Stats. http://www.thetravelingteam.org/stats, accessed September 27, 2017.

Endnotes

[78] Jordan Monson. http://www.desiringgod.org/articles/there-is-no-good-bible-for-over-a-billion-people, accessed September 26, 2017.

[79] https://www.wycliffe.org.uk/about/our-impact/, accessed July 18, 2017.

[80] https://www.goodreads.com/author/quotes/403672.Oswald_J_Smith, accessed May 4, 2017.

[81] http://biblehub.com/commentaries/calvin/matthew/9.htm, accessed May 2, 2017.

[82] http://www.thetravelingteam.org/stats/, accessed April 25, 2017.

[83] *The African Methodist Episcopal Hymn and Tune Book: Adapted to the Doctrines and Usages of the Church,* (6th ed.), Hymn #439, page 208.

[84] Andrew Murray. *With Christ in the School of Prayer.* (Peabody, Massachusetts: Hendrickson Publishers, 2007), 56.

[85] Adrian Rogers. "How to Put Power in Your Prayers," www.oneplace.com, accessed May 9, 2017.

[86] L. B. Cowman. *Streams in the Desert.* (Grand Rapids: Zondervan, 2016), March 24.

[87] Andrew Murray. *With Christ in the School of Prayer.* (Peabody, Massachusetts: Hendrickson Publishers, 2007), 55.

[88] *The Complete Works of E. M. Bounds on Prayer.* (Grand Rapids: Baker Books, 1990), Book 5, Chapter 1.

[89] L. R. Scarborough. *A Search for Souls.* (Nashville: The Sunday School Board, 1925), 15.

[90] Thomas Brooks. *Precious Remedies against Satan's Devices.* (CreateSpace Independent Publishing Platform, November 25, 2013), 144.

[91] Curtis Hutson, Ed. *Great Preaching on Prayer*. (Murfreesboro: Sword of the Lord, 1988), taken from the book jacket.

[92] J. C. Ryle. "A Call to Prayer," www.gracegems.org, accessed May 9, 2017.

[93] E. M. Bounds. *The Essentials of Prayer: Prayer and Missions.* (Dallas: Gideon House Books, 2016). Chapter 13. Bracket added by author.

[94] Ibid.

[95] A. J. Dain. *Missions Field Today.* (Chicago: Inter-Varsity Press, 1957), 15.

[96] C. H. Spurgeon. "The Secret of Power in Prayer" (sermon #2002). http://www.spurgeongems.org/vols34-36/chs2002.pdf, accessed July 3, 2017.

[97] www.navigators.org/us, accessed November 12, 2013.

[98] https://www.bestquotecollection.com/quote/leonard-ravenhill/898494, accessed May 26, 2017.

[99] C. H. Spurgeon. "Harvest Men Needed" (sermon #1127, August 17, 1873). *Metropolitan Tabernacle Pulpit.*

[100] Hyman J. Appelman. *The Savior's Invitation and Other Evangelistic Sermons.* (Grand Rapids, MI: Baker Book House, 1981), 35–42.

[101] Oswald J. Sanders. *The Revival We Need.* (New York: The Christian Alliance Publishing Company, 1925), Chapter 3.

[102] Taylor, *Why Revival Still Tarries,* 18.

Endnotes

[103] Hyman J. Appelman. *The Savior's Invitation and Other Evangelistic Sermons.* (Grand Rapids, MI: Baker Book House, 1981), 35–42.

[104] Curtis Hudson, Ed. *Great Preaching on Prayer.* (Murfreesboro, TN: Sword of the Lord Publishers, 1988), 112.

[105] Ibid., 113.

[106] Ibid.

[107] J. Oswald Sanders. *The Divine Art of Soul Winning,* 40–41.

[108] E. M. Bounds. *Power through Prayer.* https://www.biblebelievers.com/em_bounds/em-bounds_ch04.html, accessed May 1, 2017.

[109] J. C. Ryle. "A Call to Prayer," www.gracegems.org, accessed May 9, 2017.

[110] L. B. Cowman. *Streams in the Desert.* (Grand Rapids: Zondervan, 2016), March 24.

[111] Gill, John. *The New John Gill Exposition of the Entire Bible.* https://www.studylight.org/commentary/matthew/9-9.html. Commentary on Matthew 9:38, 1999.

[112] Walter A. Elwell, Philip Wesley Comfort. *Tyndale Bible Dictionary.* (Carol Stream, IL:Tyndale House Publishers, 2001), 1069.

[113] "How I Learned to Pray for the Lost" (Anonymous). http://www.btmi.org/messages/other/ilearnedpray.html, accessed June 18, 2017.

[114] C. H. Spurgeon. "Prayer—The Forerunner of Mercy," sermon #138, June 28, 1857, New Park Street Pulpit.

[115] John MacArthur. *The MacArthur Bible Commentary.* (Thomas Nelson: Nashville, 2005), 1,140.

[116] Andrew Murray. *With Christ in the School of Prayer.* (Peabody, Massachusetts: Hendrickson Publishers, 2007), 55.

[117] David Wilkerson. Pray the Lord of the Harvest (Blog). August 26, 2008. http://davidwilkersontoday.blogspot.com/2008/08/pray-lord-of-harvest.html, accessed June 20, 2017.

[118] http://www.goodreads.com/quotes/493178-men-may-spurn-our-appeals-reject-our-message-oppose-our, accessed April 25, 2017.

[119] Wesley Duwell. *Touch the World through Prayer.* (Grand Rapids: Zondervan Publishing Company, 1986), 60.

[120] John Stott, *What Christ Thinks of the Church.* (Grand Rapids, MI: Eerdmans, 1972), 111.

[121] C. H. Spurgeon. *Morning and Evening,* October 12 (morning).

[122] Warren Wiersbe. *The Bible Exposition Commentary,* Volume One. (Colorado Springs: Victor, 2001), 210.

[123] E. M. Bounds. *The Purpose of Prayer.* (CreateSpace Independent Publishing Platform, April 1, 2014), 65.

[124] Roy J. Fish and J. E. Conant. *Every Member Evangelism for Today.* (Harper & Row Publishers, 1976), 62. Cited in Bailey Smith, *Real Evangelism,* 62.

[125] http://www.kevinhalloran.net/best-e-m-bounds-christian-quotes-on-prayer/, accessed April 27, 2017.

[126] Jack Hyles. *Exploring Prayer with Jack Hyles: Praying for Laborers.* (Hammond, IN: Hyles-Anderson Publishers, 1983), Chapter 35.

[127] Ibid.

[128] Andrew Murray. *The Ministry of Intercession.* (Springdale, PA: Whitaker House, 1982), 31.

Endnotes

129 John MacArthur. "Heaven's Joy Recovering the Lost" (sermon). https://www.gty.org/library/sermons-library/42-197/heavens-joy-recovering-the-lost, accessed April 30, 2017,

130 Hyman J. Appelman. "The Saviour's Invitation." http://www.baptistbiblebelievers.com/LinkClick.aspx?fileticket=MepXWgsEa38%3D&tabid=422&mid=1341, accessed April 9, 2014.

131 Cited in R. J. Morgan. *Nelson's Annual Preacher's Sourcebook,* (2002 Edition). (Nashville: Thomas Nelson Publishers, 2001), 40.

132 C. H. Spurgeon. *The Soul Winner.* (New Kensington, PA: Whitaker House, 1995), 189.

133 C. H. Spurgeon. *Metropolitan Tabernacle Pulpit.* "A High Day in Heaven" (sermon #2791), delivered June 27, 1878.

134 Bailey Smith. *Real Evangelism.* (Nashville: Broadman Press, 1978), 153.

135 E. M. Bounds. *The Purpose of Prayer.* (CreateSpace Independent Publishing Platform, April 1, 2014).

136 "How I Learned to Pray for the Lost" (Anonymous). http://www.btmi.org/messages/other/ilearnedpray.html, accessed June 18, 2017.

137 Roger Steer. *George Müller: Delighted in God!* (Wheaton, IL: Harold Shaw, 1975), 310.

138 Andrew Murray. *School of Prayer,* (Lesson #16). http://www.fbbc.com/messages/school_of_prayer/murray_school_of_prayer_16.htm, accessed May 11, 2017.

139 *Life Invested in Punjab/Pakistan: Praying John Hyde.* http://highplacesprayer.com/index.cfm?id=d202bd33-5dc1-4473-838d76968775bef1&praying-john-hyde.html, accessed May 5, 2017.

[140] E. M. Bounds. *The Purpose of Prayer.* (CreateSpace Independent Publishing Platform, April 1, 2014), 65.

[141] E. M. Bounds. *The Purpose of Prayer.* (New York, Toronto, Chicago: Fleming H. Revell Company, 1920), 40.

[142] David Wilkerson. *Bring Your Loved Ones to Christ.* (New Jersey: Fleming Revell Company, 1979), 116.

[143] L. B. Cowman. *Streams in the Desert.* (Grand Rapids: Zondervan, 2016), May 7.

[144] Cited by C. H. Spurgeon. "True Prayer, True Power!" (sermon). http://www. theoldtimegospel.org/master/master_475.html.

[145] Jim Cymbala. "Whatever Happened to the Prayer Meeting?," http://www.heraldofhiscoming.com/Past%20Issues/2009/July/whatever_ happened_to_the_prayer_meeting.htm, accessed May 29, 2017.

[146] J. C. Ryle. "A Call to Prayer," www.gracegems.org, accessed May 9, 2017.

[147] D. L. Moody. *The Pleasure and Profit in Bible Study.* (New York: Fleming Revell Company, 1895), 94.

[148] W. A. Criswell. "Lord Teach Us to Pray" (sermon), https://www. wacriswell.com/sermons/1969/lord-teach-us-to-pray-2/, accessed May 9, 2017.

[149] http://www.epm.org/resources/2009/Mar/28/great-quotes-prayer/

[150] http://www.ccel.org/ccel/unknown/kneeling.vi.html, accessed May 5, 2017.

[151] http://www.azquotes.com/quote/544923, accessed May 15, 2017.

[152] https://daringtolivefully.com/gratitude-quotes, accessed June 1, 2017.

Endnotes

[153] http://blog.lifeway.com/newsroom/2014/10/01/new-research-americans-pray-for-friends-family-but-rarely-for-celebrities-or-sports-teams/, October 1, 2014, accessed May 28, 2017.

[154] C. H. Spurgeon. *Metropolitan Tabernacle Pulpit.* "The Secret of Power in Prayer," (sermon #2002), January 8, 1888.

[155] C. H. Spurgeon. *Only a Prayer Meeting.* (Great Britain: Christian Focus Publications, 2000), 21.

[156] Ibid., 20.

[157] Leonard Ravenhill. *Why Revival Tarries.* (Bloomington, Minnesota: Bethany Publishing House, 1987), 19, 21.

[158] Jim Cymbala. "Whatever Happened to the Prayer Meeting?," http://www.heraldofhiscoming.com/Past%20Issues/2009/July/whatever_happened_to_the_prayer_meeting.htm, accessed May 29, 2017.

[159] http://www.gospeltruth.net/ravenhill.htm, accessed May 30, 2017.

[160] Jerry Rankin. *To the Ends of the Earth.* (Nashville: B & H Publishers, 2006), 69.

[161] C. H. Spurgeon. *Only a Prayer Meeting.* (Great Britain: Christian Focus Publications, 2000), 9.

[162] Bengel's Gnomen, Matthew 9:38. http://biblehub.com/commentaries/matthew/9-38.htm, accessed July 3, 2017.

[163] http://www.liveatthewell.org/quotes-from-corrie-ten-boom.html, accessed May 28, 2017.

[164] David Wilkerson. "The Harvest Instruments," http://www.sermonindex.net/modules/newbb/viewtopic.php?topic_id=56147&forum=45, accessed June 24, 2017.

[165] W. W. Wiersbe. *Be Decisive.* (Wheaton, IL: Victor Books, 1996), 84.

[166] Robert G. Lee. *Sermonic Library: Seven Swords.* (Orlando, FL: Christ for the World Publishers, 1981), 53–56.

[167] Arthur Bennett, Ed., *The Valley of Vision.* (Carlisle, PA: The Banner of Truth, 2002), 320–321.

[168] http://www.azquotes.com/quotes/topics/soul-winning.html, accessed December 14, 2017.

[169] http://www.kevinhalloran.net/best-e-m-bounds-christian-quotes-on-prayer/, accessed April 27, 2017.